To Liz,

I hope you enjoy

meeting these incredible

women!

Rita M Glaze

'2004

LifeLines ©

Stories from Women with Hope

LifeLines
Stories from
WOMEN
With HOPE

RITA GLAZE

Intuitive
ih
Health

CHICAGO

LifeLines© - Stories of Women with Hope
Intuitive Health, Inc.
2003

Intuitive Health hardcover edition published April 2003

Cover and Book Design by Karen Sawyer
Back Cover Photo courtesy of Nancy Stratinsky
Edited by Mike Yorkey

Library of Congress Cataloging-in-Publication Data
Glaze, Rita
LifeLines: Stories From Women With Hope/Rita Glaze
p. cm.
ISBN 0-9740401-1-8 (hardcover)
2003105349

Printed in the United States of America

This book is dedicated to the women who are searching for comfort and the people who love them . . . your LifeLines© are here.

To the women who shared their stories, we thank you for your courage, honesty, sincerity and hope. You are true heroes.

To my own personal 'LifeLines', I am forever grateful for the connection, strength, joy and humor that you have brought to my life.

The future belongs to those who believe in the beauty of their dreams.

- Eleanor Roosevelt

Contents

Acknowledgements

This dream could not have become a reality without the love, dedication and support of so many people throughout my life. I am forever grateful to...

My family: Iris, Randy, Nancy, Reneé, Shelley, Ron, Ruth, Dave, Ron, Tony, Ryan & Danny for always being my safe harbor and my greatest loves.

Wally (my dad in heaven): Thank you for making me in your likeness; I wish you were here to see this, you would have loved it.

Rudie: For sharing my voice and always enriching my spirit.

My 'Girls': Cherylyn, Kristin and Lori, who taught me everything there is to know about true friendship, life, love, and loyalty.

Doctors Perlman & Wynn: who take great care of my mind and my body and who helped to guide me on my path to rediscovering my spirit and my voice.

Eric, for always believing in me and making me reach for my dreams. Rock Steady, my friend.

Robert, for teaching me that people always want to be part of something special.

Acknowledgements

All of my friends and extended family, for supporting me, cheering for me and always being enthusiastic, even when it probably sounded like I had lost my mind, again!

Karen for her creative spirit, dedication, hard work and grace in putting this book together.

Thom for his insight and incredible talent in helping me envision this project.

Sherill for her incredible energy, expertise, tenacity and constant inspiration.

Dan for his medical support, talent and experience in making this series a reality.

Preface

As we move through our lives, there are many moments when our strength and courage are tested. One such moment is when we face a life-changing illness. These instances shake our foundation and require us to heal both our bodies and our spirits. Sometimes this can happen simultaneously and other times, it is a longer process. No matter how long our process takes, we learn something from these experiences. These experiences mold us into the people we are today.

Dealing with a serious illness can leave you with overwhelming feelings of uncertainty and anxiety. The process of diagnosis and treatment can be filled with information overload and decision making that none of us are prepared for at the time. But facing a life-changing illness is more than just doctors, diagnostics, medications and procedures. There is a human experience that surrounds each of us as we go through our medical experience.

The human experience is everything that

happens outside of the doctor's office. The human experience is the relationship that we develop with our disease. The human experience is how our relationships change based on how illness affects us now. It is how our lifestyles need to be adjusted with our new set of circumstances and how our vantage point changes from the other side of an illness. It becomes our point of view from which we now see our lives. It is our view of the world. It is our view from the side of a cure or remission or successful management of a condition.

I was diagnosed with multiple sclerosis in February of 2002. I had been working in the healthcare industry for ten years so I was no stranger to disease and pharmaceutical information. This was my career. I had access to any information that I wanted. Scientific literature and any other source that you could think of, I could get my hands on. What I realized was information wasn't what I needed. I needed to hear the stories of others. I needed to know the human side.

The way that I learned the human side was asking and listening to other women's stories. From these stories, I learned an important lesson. That lesson was that all of our experiences had a similar voice. While our diseases may be different, our experiences shared a voice. We were a sisterhood, of sorts. We spoke a similar language. If I could learn from these voices, then so could many other women who may be facing what I did.

Thus, the idea for LifeLines© was born. LifeLines©: Stories From Women With Hope are stories shared by women who have faced life-changing illnesses. These stories are written in their own voices, from their own view of the world. They are meant to provide comfort, connection and support to women and those who love them. For anyone who may be facing what we have, our hope is to provide you with a place to turn to when you need to hear someone with the same voice.

My Story

My name is Rita. I am a 35 year old single professional woman. In 2002, I was diagnosed with multiple sclerosis (MS).

I was like so many other single professional women in their early 30s. I was chasing the dream. You know that fantasy we all talk about. The successful career woman who can leap tall corporate structures in a single bound while trying to find a meaningful relationship and be the life of the party when she wants to be. Yeah. That's the one. I remember in my late twenties my best friends had nicknamed me "Corporate Diva". I wore that title proudly for quite some time.

Work for me was a rush. I had the chance to work with incredibly bright, talented people who continually challenged and inspired me. That was my driving force. It was where I derived my energy and inspiration. I was after constant intellectual challenge. If there was an assignment no one else wanted, I volunteered - even if I didn't understand what to do first or whom to call. I just figured it out as I went along.

I attribute it to my love of sports. I grew up playing them. I was always part of a team and developed a deep sense of competition. I think being part of a big family helped too. There are five siblings in my family, of which I am the youngest. We all have the same spirit. It builds your sense of team at an early age. If not your sense of team, at least your survival skills in a group setting. It prepared me for many of the meetings I would have in my corporate career. In some respects, the dynamics were the same.

My sense of competition and drive were the qualities that had raised me up to where I wanted to be. I never realized they were my Achilles' heel. My time of discovery was right around the corner.

It began in November of 2001. During that time, I held a high level position in an agency. The agency did specialized work in the healthcare industry. I was located in Chicago and most of my clients were on the

East Coast. I was traveling about 50% of the time meeting with clients. When I wasn't with clients, I was in the office managing a staff of about four people. On average, I worked between 50-55 hours a week. I had been with the agency about a year and it was going great. I liked my job. I had settled into my role, learned the environment, made some friends and was getting ready to take on a new account.

I was watching TV on a Sunday evening when I noticed the vision in my right eye was a little blurry. I wear contacts so I wasn't too concerned. I thought they needed to be cleaned. I took them out, cleaned them up and went to bed. I noticed when I woke up the next day that even with my glasses on I was having the same problem. I still wasn't overly concerned since I had an optometrist appointment scheduled for Wednesday afternoon.

For the next two days, the vision in my right eye steadily diminished. It became more blurry. As my vision became more distorted, the headaches began. It became difficult for me to concentrate and function. I was working on a computer all day - researching, reading and writing - so being visually impaired was a challenge. I kept thinking, "Wednesday will be here, he will figure out what's wrong and that will be it." Deep down, I knew that it wouldn't be that easy.

Wednesday arrived and I went to my optometrist.

"There is nothing on the surface of your eye that has been damaged or infected," he said. "There is a problem, but it must be something further back than I can see with the equipment that I have here."

He referred me to a neuroophthalmologist whom he called from his office, while I was sitting in the chair. He made my appointment for first thing the next morning.

When I arrived on Thursday morning, my vision was still in decline and my head was now pounding from the headache. The ophthalmologist did an initial eye exam and dilation tests. He concluded that I was probably suffering from optic neuritis. Optic neuritis is inflammation somewhere along the optic nerve. The only way to be sure was for me to have an MRI of my brain. The MRI would pinpoint the inflammation. He also told me that these symptoms could be consistent with multiple sclerosis (MS). He handed me the name of a neurologist that he highly recommended. He said that I should make an appointment with him once I had my MRI results.

That was the first time that I had heard the words me and multiple sclerosis coupled in the same sentence, but I really didn't think about it at the time. I got up out of the chair, thanked Dr. Berman and left his office. I called my brother, sister and sister-in-law to give them the update from my cell phone and drove to the office. At the office, I did some research on the statistics of optic neuritis and MS. I was going to be prepared. The latest article stated that approximately 30% of patients with optic neuritis were later diagnosed with MS. I knew this was a reasonable link and a fairly high percentage. I started to get nervous.

I scheduled my MRI for the next day. I was thankful that my brother, Randy and his wife, Nancy, were there with me. They joked with me in the waiting room. My family has always been able to use humor to cope with many situations and this was no different. This was my first medical experience. At 33, I had never been through anything other than routine OB/GYN visits. Little did I know that I was in for a whole host of new experiences, more than I would be able to handle.

It was a couple of days later when Dr. Berman, the ophthalmologist, called me with the results. He told me that my results were 'similar to that of MS', but he wanted me to seek the counsel of the neurologist for a definitive diagnosis. In my mind, I felt like I had to start adjusting to the fact that I probably had MS. Meanwhile, I still had blurry vision and headaches. The next day, I scheduled my first appointment with the neurologist that has treated me ever since, Dr. Wynn.

My first appointment with Dr. Wynn is one that I will never forget. He sat with me and my sister-in-law, Nancy, and talked with us for over an hour. He explained all of my symptoms and what they meant. He told me that it could very well be MS. My MRI showed that I had lesions. I had the 'right number' and they were the 'right size' to meet the diagnostic criteria. What he didn't do was rush to diagnose me with MS. What he did do, was rush to treat my sight. He gave me a perspective which was important for me to have then and I still carry with me today. That perspective was that having or not having MS wasn't going to matter so much that day as it was for me to 'see' so I could go on about my life.

Believe me, it is so much easier to look back and recall that lesson than it was to learn it as I went. That day, he told me that the way to treat the inflammation of my optic nerve was with steroids. In my head, I thought great, write me a prescription. I don't want to be on steroids, but I want to have my vision back soon. Not so fast. The steroids would have to be given intravenously (IV). On top of that, since I had never been on IV steroids before, I would have to go into the hospital for three days to make sure that I was monitored appropriately.

My head went right to the office. I thought, "I have too much work to do. Now this is getting in the way."

As crazy as it was, I was trying to figure out how I was going to go back to work and tell them that I was going into the hospital. The next day was Friday. I figured I could check into the hospital on Friday afternoon and be out by Sunday afternoon. I could be back to work on Monday. Another first for me - beginning to explain to my employer, that my availability may not be 24/7. It was more of a shock for me than it was for them. Everything went well and I was back in the office on Monday morning.

Over the next few months, I would face many 'firsts'. I had my first hospital stay; my first IV; my first round of prescriptions; my first experiences with self-injections; and, my first lessons in educating my friends, family and coworkers on what it meant to have MS. I am a very open person, so I didn't have a problem educating people on my disease.

Disease education had been part of my career, so explaining complex disease information was the easy part for me. The complicated part came when people started asking me questions about how this would affect me. Those were questions I didn't have any answers to at the time. I was living under the assumption that I could go on with the life that I was leading and somehow fit this in. I was under the impression that "good players played hurt", so like a good player, I would just get back on the field.

Since December, I had been feeling good. Working hard and feeling like I had a good handle on everything. It wasn't until the second week in February when things started to slip away. I noticed one night that my left leg felt 'numb' when I went to rest my arm on it. This wasn't a good sign.

Within two days, the numbness had spread up my left leg, into my groin area. By the third day, it was all the way up my back. You could have drawn a line down my body and I wouldn't have been able to feel anything on the left side of that line. The only good news was that it never spread into my arm. I called Dr. Wynn's office, described my symptoms and was told to come to the office Thursday at 5:00 p.m. It was the first available appointment. That was only two days away. I could wait that long. I was only putting off the inevitable. He was going to tell me that I 'officially' had MS.

I arrived in Dr. Wynn's office at 5:00 p.m. on February 14, 2002. I was in the waiting room for about 45 minutes. It was then that I realized the irony of the term waiting room. There I was, 'waiting' for my life to change. I knew that when I came back through this waiting room, my life wouldn't be the same.

There would be a new set of information, a new set of labels and probably a new set of rules for my life.

There would be a new language that I would have to understand and that I would have to teach my family and friends. I was going to need to understand how difficult that was going to be for them. When I came back out of the exam room, the waiting room looked exactly the same. It hadn't changed and neither had I from hearing those words. Those changes would take a bit longer, but they were inevitable.

It was official. I drove home that night and made the necessary phone calls to inform my family and close friends that my 'official' diagnosis had come. I didn't feel any different. I realized that I had already been living the life of an MS patient for the past three months. I didn't need to hear the words to make it real. I was already there. I went home and slept well that night. I had to take care of the current problem, the numbness on my left side. We had a fix for that.

Back on the IV steroids, this time with home health care, which was another first. This would fit much better into my lifestyle. They would come to my home and administer the IV and I would go on about my day. That is, I would go to work. I would wrap my hand in an ace bandage to cover the IV shunt and then go to the office. I would conduct client meetings and get my job done. When people asked, I would tell them that I sprained my wrist. I would push past this, it was just temporary. That is what I kept telling myself.

I kept pushing on. The months past and my schedule continued to be as grueling as it had always been. I was traveling from one side of the country to the other, working to serve my clients and the agency. When asked to take on another new client in April, I agreed. It was going to be a tremendous undertaking, but I had done it before and this wouldn't be any different. My ego was writing checks that my body couldn't cash.

It wasn't until late July of 2002, that it all started to come crashing down. The left side of my body, which in February had been numb, had come back to life in March and was now in pain. As my stress and fatigue levels escalated, so did my pain. While desperately trying to hold on to life as I knew it, my body revolted. The pain was so bad one day, that my body shut down to the point where I couldn't get out of bed. I woke up and the left side of my body was in so much deep pain that I couldn't move.

It was a Friday morning. On my plate that day was finishing an assignment and getting ready for a flight on Monday morning to meet with my new client. All I felt was sheer terror and excruciating pain. By the time I could reach the phone to call the office, they were already calling me. When I heard the HR director's voice on the other end of the phone, I was in tears. I had finally met my limit. They cancelled all of my meetings for the next couple of days.

The next few days were spent resting and trying to regain a sense of myself. After a few days, I realized that I wasn't going to be able to do that alone. I placed a call to Dr. Wynn.

After meeting with him, I decided to take some time off from my job to truly recover, both physically and emotionally. I also started to work with a therapist to help me discover how to make clear choices about my life and my disease, both large and small.

My absence from the agency lasted for five weeks. In those five weeks I made many discoveries about myself. I discovered that I needed to make choices every day about my energy and how precious it was to me. For me, with MS, there are two factors that I confront everyday - pain and fatigue. The more tired I get, the more pain I have. I had to learn that energy is my life's currency. I had to learn to make choices about where I would spend my energy. That doesn't include only physical energy, but emotional energy too. That was the hardest lesson for me. I had to start making hard decisions on where my energy and passion were going to be spent.

During my leave of absence, I spent a lot of time

with my family and friends who have been my strongest sense of connection and support for my entire life. They helped me to see the joys that I had in my life and those that I was missing. They have always been there to provide me with the comfort and safety that I craved. It was an important journey for me and I was glad to have them all with me as I took that trip.

I also did a lot of writing in my journal. It helped me to relieve anxiety about what I was going through. It also helped me to rediscover my voice. When I went back to work in mid September, I felt like a different person. I was able to set boundaries for myself and decide what was important for me. I was also able to look at my life from a new perspective. I also realized that the energy that it took for me to excel at my position, in that environment, was more than I was willing to give. It wasn't a trade off that I was willing to make anymore. The agency and I didn't seem to fit together anymore. I left the agency in December of 2002.

I made the decision to leave the agency because I craved a different kind of connection now than I had before. What I wanted to do was to show people that there is another side to having a disease. There is more to this experience than a diagnosis, a treatment or a prognosis. There is emotion, passion, relationships and learning that are important and come out of these experiences. In my case, what I learned about myself was important. I have learned more about who I am and who I want to be in the last year, than I think I would have in the next ten years had I not had this experience. I also learned how to rebuild my life in a way that is positive for me and for the people who love me.

In some ways, I wish there was a different way I could have learned these lessons. But if that would have happened, I would not be where I am today. I would not be able to share with you the 13 amazing and inspirational stories that you are about to read.

In the following chapters, you will meet the courageous women of LifeLines©.

These women have faced incredible challenges in their lives and have graciously come forward to share their stories. These stories capture the bravery, hope and courage each woman exhibits in dealing with her disease and her life. These women are truly inspiring, not only in sharing their stories to help other women, but in their courage to thrive in their own lives.

What is my hope?

I have always believed that we learn and teach from our experiences. In the past year and a half, I learned a great deal from other people who faced similar circumstances in their lives. Some were friends, some were family members and others were people that I met through my own diagnosis. What I learned was that we experience moments in a similar way and we can all learn and teach through these connections to each other. My hope is that LifeLines© may bring some of these connections to you and those you love. As you or your family may be facing a life-changing illness, my true hope is that you connect with one of us or all of us to find comfort and support.

Holly's Story

Holly, 36, is a married, professional woman. In 1998, she was diagnosed with acute lymphocytic leukemia (ALL).

It's hard not to smile when I think about what my life used to be like. Come on, I was a successful thirty-one-year-old married career woman. My husband and I filled every minute of every day with something. We worked hard and played harder. I was an accountant for an international accounting firm and we loved to travel. I can't count all the weekends we spent in New York or Washington D.C. Somewhere we had bought into the notion that if you busted your tail off in your job, then you deserved to pamper yourself.

Once I was on a two-year project that was so grueling that it felt like it soaked up every minute that I had. It wasn't unusual for me to work straight through the night a couple of times a week. I looked back at our calendar one year and realized that we had been gone every single weekend somewhere with our friends.

Every single weekend.

That's why I was so unprepared for July of 1998. I was working on a project in Texas, and the heat was sweltering. One evening I felt light-headed and I thought I was dehydrated due to the high temperatures. A few days later I flew home. I couldn't wait to get outside for my morning walk, which was a three-mile route. About halfway through the course, I felt the same sensation I had felt in Texas—nausea and a little dizziness. I drank some water and kept walking. I was sure it was the heat again.

It was by coincidence that the next week I was having an outpatient procedure performed at a local hospital. I had been diagnosed with endometriosis and needed to have a laparoscopy to remove endometrial tissue.

Even though it was an outpatient procedure, they still wanted to put me under general anesthesia. While I was waiting to be wheeled into surgery, the anesthesiologist walked up to my bed—holding my chart—and asked, "Did you know you were anemic?"

I turned my head to face her. "No," I said. "Are you sure?"

She shook her head. "You are anemic, and we need to understand why. If you weren't an otherwise healthy thirty-one-year-old, there is no way we would do this procedure. We are going to go ahead with it and figure out why you're anemic later."

When I woke up, they told me that they wound up performing an oophorectomy, which involves the removal of an ovary. When they went in through the laparoscope, they found a cyst that was too large to remove, so they had to make an incision about six inches long to remove the ovary. Because of my anemia, they gave me several units of blood during the procedure.

I wasn't going anywhere until they could figure out why I was anemic. My husband was on his way back from a business trip that had taken him out of the country. He landed that evening and was right there by my side. Earlier that day I had called my mother, who lives in Nebraska. When she heard what was happening, she was on a plane to Richmond, VA. She knew that something wasn't right and she was going to be there with me. That is how it works in my family. It really is "all for one and one for all".

A hematologist showed up and started running tests

including a bone marrow biopsy. It was important for me to understand the range of possibilities. The best case was that I was simply anemic. The worst case was that I had leukemia.

And just like that, my life changed forever.

"You have leukemia," he said.

"I have what?" I asked. I didn't really know what leukemia was.

After the disease was explained to me, I think I went into a little bit of shock. They kept me in for three days because they had to keep giving me blood. My hemoglobin levels were so low that the only way they could get them back up was through transfusions. I was referred to an academic medical center because they would be better equipped to offer me options. I checked out on Tuesday and drove to my appointment at the medical center with my mom and my husband on Wednesday.

My new doctor didn't mince any words.

"You have leukemia, and you need a bone marrow transplant," he said. And that wasn't all.

"If you were my daughter, I would want you to come home and be near your family and take care of your personal matters and do it right away," he said quietly.

I remember sitting there not being able to

comprehend what he was telling me.

"When you say 'right away,'" I questioned, "do you mean next week right away?"

The doctor shook his head.

"No, tonight right away," he said. "You need to be on that plane tonight."

How do I describe what goes on in your head when your world feels like its getting flipped upside down? I remember trying desperately to focus, feeling a need to pay attention to the detail that was going on around me. Somehow I felt like I would be able to get through this thing if I could process each moment as it came.

The next day we packed everything we could haul out on short notice, threw my medical records together, and headed home for Nebraska. When my husband's company heard what was happening, they volunteered the use of their corporate jet, which made our trip easier to take. We left Richmond, Virginia at 7 a.m. Friday morning, and we were at the medical center in Nebraska by one o'clock in the afternoon. The center was near my parent's home in Nebraska, but my three sisters and brother flew in from around the country to be with me during my consultation. Whatever the mystery was that was waiting for me out there, it was going to have to go through my family to get to me.

The doctors did another bone marrow biopsy that

confirmed the diagnoses and found that 95 percent of my cells were leukemia cells.

"You have no time," I was told. "You need a bone marrow transplant now, and we'll have to match you with a donor."

Since all my family was at arm's length, they lined up to be tested as possible donors. My older sister Jill was found to be a match. Two days later, on July 27th, I went into the hospital. I didn't come out until just before Christmas. It took that long to get me into remission and ready for the transplant. I was able to be home for Christmas for a few weeks, but I returned in mid-January with my sister Jill for the transplant.

It was such a tough thing. After five days of high dose chemotherapy and full body radiation—which basically wiped out my body—they gave me the bone marrow and then started counting the days. It was so strange. They began by counting down the days until the transplant: Negative 5, Negative 4, Negative 3, Negative 2, Negative 1, and then 0—the day of the transplant. Then they started counting the days I survived: Day 1, Day 2, and Day 3. These were called milestone days. I didn't realize it at the time, but they were counting the days that I was alive. I remember Day 100 was a big celebration.

Later on I would recall the first time I was in my

doctor's office. He had asked everybody to leave so that he could be alone with me. He just wanted to talk. I remembered thinking that this would be my chance to get some real answers.

"Give it to me straight, doctor," I said. "I need to know. What are my chances here? How long do you think I have?"

He leaned over and looked me straight in the eyes. "My job is to heal you," he said. "And I am going to do everything I can to heal you."

Each time I asked him, he would always tell me the same thing. "My job is to heal you, and that is what I intend to do."

A few years later, he told me that if he would have been honest with me that day, he would have given me a 2 to 3 percent chance of surviving. Hearing that was the first time I knew how sick I really had been.

There is nothing that can prepare you for a struggle of such immense proportions. The hope I offer you is that you will be surprised how deep your personal resources are and how strong you are deep down. And your desire to live will be like a furnace from which you will draw your energy.

It's okay to be confused. I think it takes a while to figure out what's coming at you. Don't be afraid of reaching out to whatever family gives your life meaning.

Experiencing my family's love and support when I needed it most was the greatest gift of all.

I'm back working full time again. We moved back to Richmond after my husband was offered a promotion. I find myself wondering what would happen if my leukemia would ever come back, but I can't worry too much about it. I can't live my life wondering if I will get sick again. We dealt with it once and if it happens, we will deal with it again. Now we know that we have the strength to get through anything together. All I can do is keep my priorities straight and do what a normal thirty-six-year-old woman would do.

Live each day.

What is our hope?

Holly is a true example of the healing power of a patient's spirit. There are many "places" we can go to feed our spirits when they are weakened. Sometimes, we find they come to us when we need them most. The two sources that are most evident in Holly's story are her family and her doctor. The devotion of Holly's husband and family to focus on her care, healing and support makes me realize how important it is to surround ourselves with those people who can continuously encourage our healing. The focus of Holly's doctor on empowering her journey back to health was a powerful force in her recovery. It reminds me that sometimes the focus is not on how sick we are, but on how well we will be.

Becka's Story

Becka, 40, is a married, professional woman raising two children. In 2002, she was diagnosed with celiac disease and peripheral neuropathy.

We are an active family of four. We seemed like the family that you see in TV commercials, always on the go. We were everywhere. It was wonderful. Our kids were involved in lots of activities. As a couple, we were very socially active. We went out to dinner, movies and spent time with our friends. We also spent time traveling. It was part of our make up to be active and social. It's part of who we are as a family.

Individually, I was always on the move. I always exercised and walking was my exercise of choice. It gave me an outlet to keep me healthy and clear my head. My walks were brisk. I had a regular route around the neighborhood. It was a great way for me to get ready for the day ahead.

My days are filled with structured chaos, some might call it. I have a day care service. During the day, I care for fifteen children in my home. It is filled with teaching and learning for everyone. It is a demanding job with activities and structured timing to provide a safe, nurturing and fun environment for these children. It provides a deep sense of fulfillment for me. Some days it could stretch me physically, so in March of 2002 when I first noticed some bruises on my arms, I didn't take it too seriously.

Within about a week, I discovered that I had about 10-15 bruises on my arms and legs, I took it more seriously. My husband and I drove to a research hospital, which was about an hour away. There we met with a hematologist to see if we could gain some insight into what was happening. He ran some basic tests and everything came back negative. Everything seemed to be okay.

It wasn't until about two months later, in May, when things started to escalate. I was out for a brisk walk. I was about a half a block from our house, when I just kind of collapsed. When I regained myself and made it back to the house, I told my husband that I felt like I was coming down with the flu. I went to my doctor. After examining me, his opinion was that I was coming down with some kind of virus.

After about a week, I didn't seem to be getting any better. I was feeling worse. I was feeling new symptoms. These were burning sensations. They would travel up from my feet, through my leg and up my thigh. It was like someone turned me upside down and was pouring hot water on my feet and letting it flow up my leg. When I went back to the doctor, he referred me to a neurologist. We drove the hour to the research hospital to see him.

The neurologist that I was referred to was the head of the department. I thought that I would receive some quick answers. While I was there, he did some peripheral nerve tests which check for nerve injury. He also mentioned that it could be symptoms related to multiple sclerosis (MS). With the mention of multiple sclerosis, he wanted to put my mind at ease and run some tests to rule that out. I went through several tests including an eye exam and other MS-related neurological exams. They all came back negative. By end of the day, he patted me on the back and said he thought for sure it was a virus. He told me I was fine and that it would go away.

It didn't go away and I wasn't fine. I steadily got worse. My joints became swollen and achy. I developed a rash all over me. I started to feel as if there was a huge weight on me and I couldn't move. It was weakening me. As May came to a close, I was not climbing out of this fog, but getting more and more lost. I went searching for help.

My daughter's pediatrician, who had become a friend of our family, suggested that I go to another MS center for evaluation. Given the symptoms that I was currently displaying, the possibility of MS was once again looming over us. I was able to secure an appointment at the Cleveland Clinic with their MS specialists. The clinic didn't have the availability to schedule all of the tests that I needed at one time. When I was there, I was able to have most of my tests run. But, I was going to have to go back in a couple of weeks for the rest. Little did I know, I wouldn't be able to wait that long.

Within a week of returning from the Cleveland Clinic, I went quickly downhill. I couldn't make it from the couch to the chair. I was in so much pain. It felt like someone had put Ben-Gay® all over my body and then rubbed my skin with a scouring pad. It felt like that all over my body. I could barely function. My family had to do everything for me. I was sinking into a deep depression. Here I was fading away and no one seemed to know why. How much further would I sink? Would it be until I completely disappeared?

Meanwhile, the question of MS was still looming over me. I completed the last of the tests including a spinal tap, a test that consists of removing fluid from your spinal canal for evaluation and MRI scans of my brain and spine to check for lesions. Those tests all came back negative. All of the doctors around here seemed to be scratching their heads. Again I turned to my friend and my daughter's doctor for help. He knew of a physician at the Mayo Clinic and thought it might be worth a shot.

I was able to get an appointment that same month, which was a feat in itself. I was scheduled for late in June. We flew to Minnesota and stayed there for four days. I saw a number of specialists to try to find answers and comfort. Shuttling from office to office with dermatologists, infectious disease specialists, hematologists and neurologists and no one seemed to have anything new to tell me. The only new information was that I had small fiber neuropathy. The doctors, at this point, couldn't determine what had caused my condition. They were going to prescribe me a different medication. It was time for lunch and then my last exam.

I had finished lunch and proceeded to my last exam.

It was a neurology exam and it was with a different neurologist than I had seen before. In the last hour since lunch, I had swollen up pretty bad.

"Have you seen a rheumatologist while you have been here?" he said.

"No," I said.

Surprisingly, that was the one specialist I had not met on my trip to Minnesota. My next appointment was in rheumatology. After she examined me, the rheumatologist explained to me that I didn't have any rheumatic problems, but she noticed something in my lab report. I had tested positive for a particular antibody. She confirmed with me that I hadn't seen a gastroenterologist and made an appointment for me.

I was at my wit's end, so what was one more appointment. About an hour later, I was in the office of the head of the celiac unit at the Mayo Clinic. After answering a number of questions, he informed me that there may be a 30% chance that I may have celiac disease. The best way to determine if you have the disease is through a biopsy. Three hours later, I was prepped for an endoscopy. During the endoscopy, doctors inserted a tube down through my throat, which has a tiny camera on the end to guide them through the esophagus, the stomach and to the small intestines where they took a small tissue sample for evaluation. I was exhausted from the experience. That night we made the long drive home.

Then the waiting began. I was still exhausted from all of the tests and still had no relief from my symptoms. I was feeling worse and worse, both physically and emotionally. I was completely depressed. It was the Fourth of July weekend and I was feeling like I had nothing to celebrate. I was losing my independence to an unseen enemy. What was going to happen next?

Monday morning came and the phone rang to bring me the news. The doctor called to tell me I had celiac disease. My biopsy had come back positive for the disease. Finally an answer! Unfortunately, the answer came on July 7, 2002, my 40th birthday. What a way to ring in a new decade. Little did I know what would come next.

Celiac disease occurs when a body reacts abnormally to gluten which is a protein found in wheat, rye, barley and oats. The gluten causes an inflammatory response in the small intestine which damages the tissues and can impair a body's ability to absorb nutrients from foods. In my case, my intestines were so stripped that my body was literally attacking other organs looking for nutrients. Hence, my other symptoms.

I had my answers and I had a plan. I immediately started my new diet. Within a week, I felt like a new person. All of the swelling went down and the rash disappeared. My energy level shot right back up. My old self was starting to emerge, once again. The new diet was something that I could control. It was a challenge, but I could see the progress already. It was going to be difficult, but I could do it.

My whole lifestyle had to change. It is amazing when you are faced with something like this how much you have to learn in a short amount of time. At first, I thought I would have to make different food choices. As I started to research my condition, I realized that this was not going to be just about food, but about everything in my lifestyle. Gluten is a protein found in wheat. Wheat is found in more places than I ever imagined. It affected every aspect of my lifestyle from my lipstick, toothpaste, gum, deodorant and perfume choices.

Our household runs differently now. We have literally two separate kitchens in our house. One for Mom and one for the rest of the family. I have a separate toaster, utensils, pots and pans along with special food. It is all marked with 'MOM's' stickers. It has been a difficult adjustment since the first time I met with the dietician. That day I felt like I was thrown into a whirlwind. As I learned more, I felt more comfortable. I also have a book that helps me through what brands are gluten-free and "safe" for me. If I didn't have that, I don't know what I would do sometimes.

It is still difficult for me at times. Grocery shopping is a challenge. I shop at a gluten-free store which is about an hour away from our house. It is also much more expensive than shopping at a regular grocery store. A gluten-free loaf of bread is about five times the price of a regular loaf of bread. I also found some places to order gluten-free products through the internet. If I am nothing else, I am persistent.

That is true of my search for the right doctor. After my diagnosis I searched for the kind of doctor who could give me answers. I had celiac disease but I also had peripheral neuropathy. It wasn't a widely seen combination, but that didn't mean I was going to settle. I did my research and found a doctor at Cornell University in New York who was doing research in patients with my two conditions. I spoke to him, felt comfortable and made an appointment. Now I fly to New York to get specialized care from someone who understands what I need.

My most recent appointment in December went very well. I had another biopsy. The results indicated that my small intestines are healing. My gluten levels are within normal range. As long as I stay gluten-free, I will stay in remission. That is a good feeling. The neuropathy is a little more challenging. That is a day-to-day management with medication, but I seem to be making progress there too.

I even started to reach out to other celiac patients. I recently came across five people in my area that had been recently diagnosed with the disease. It started me thinking about support. The nearest support group for me was 90 miles away. I contacted the nearby celiac Foundation and asked them to perform a search for me. They searched for anyone in the United States who had Celiac disease and neuropathy. From that search, we had four responses. We started our own support group. Our first meeting was held at the end of March, 2003.

Support was what I was given from my family. They have always been just where I needed them, by my side. My husband has been 'my rock'. He has always had a positive attitude and stood beside me. Even when I felt my worst, he was always telling me we would get through it. Our relationship is much closer now. My two children were the same way. They were scared, but they were very understanding and caring. There were days when my 13-year-old son would not leave my side. He just wanted to take care of me. As a family, I think we are all closer and that feels good. We made it through together.

I am on the move again. My life, while it may look a bit different from the outside, is still rich in all that matters. While there may be a little less spontaneity in our lives, we have everything that is important, each other.

What is our hope?

Becka tells us the story of change from every aspect of rebuilding your life from the 'inside out'. Struggling to find answers while you feel yourself slip away is a painful experience for anyone. Once she found answers to her questions, a new challenge arose for her. She could not imagine the choices that she would have to make in every aspect of her lifestyle just to stay healthy. She not only made the choices, but reached out to others as well. In establishing a support group for people with her same conditions, she will find support and be able to give support to others. Thank you, Becka for your inspiration.

. . . Rita

Barb's Story

---

*Barb, 46, is a divorced,
professional woman with two
children. At 29, she suffered a stroke.*

Someone should make a movie about life at twenty-nine. My life back in 1985 had it going from every angle. I was working on the second year of my marriage. I had finished up all my coursework for my Ph.D. in Clinical Psychology and was just coming out of my internship. I was finished collecting my data and was working on my outline for my dissertation on body image in children. Finishing school was proving to be a handful.

Wherever I could squeeze it in, I worked full time in a hospital psychiatric ward. I was logging in about fifty hours a week of family counseling, which put me in touch with all kinds of people. Whatever free time I had left, I would go horseback riding or do a little reading and writing on the side.

It was a Sunday in June when things started to change. I woke up that morning experiencing a noise in my right ear that sounded like a helicopter landing on my shoulder. Throughout the day I was having brief episodes with the roar, which was something I had never had before. I felt like I was having trouble swallowing, which was more than a little unusual. I also felt some dizziness.

The next day, I made an appointment to see an ear, nose, and throat specialist at the hospital. Based on my symptoms, he couldn't give me a clear diagnosis. The exam didn't show anything. Everything seemed normal.

"If it happens again," the doctor said, "I suggest you go to the emergency room." He gave me medication for my dizziness. I went to bed knowing I had done my duty by going to the doctor. Everything would be all right.

I awoke the next morning, and it was clear something was seriously wrong. I lay in bed trying to focus my thoughts, but I was finding it impossible to think clearly. I remember knowing I was home alone because my husband was out of town. But for some reason, I couldn't get myself physically out of bed. I could wiggle my toes. I thought that if I could just lay there and wiggle my toes, I would be all right. I was not thinking clearly.

I lay in bed almost the entire day, wiggling my toes.

Around three o'clock in the afternoon, my head started to clear. I began to comprehend that something was wrong with me and I wasn't getting any better. The phone rang and it was my sister-in-law from out of state. It was at that point that I realized that I couldn't speak. I managed to push out some words like "arm", "leg" and "can't", but it was the best I could do. My sister-in-law knew immediately that I was in trouble and she told me to call the paramedics, but I couldn't manage the call. She hung up and called 911 for me.

By the time the paramedics arrived I had figured out how to get myself out of bed. I leaned on one wall and then the next until I had managed to get myself dressed and the front door unlocked. My motor skills on my right side had disappeared. I shuffled around the house and managed to feed the cats and get some phone numbers together before the paramedics pulled up. My sister-in-law had told me on the phone that I may be having a cerebral hemorrhage. I knew I might be gone for a while.

When we arrived at the hospital around four that afternoon, it was clear that I was having a stroke. The ER team needed to run a CAT scan, but the hospital's equipment was broken so I was transferred to another hospital. My brother and in-laws met me there and waited outside while they ran tests for about eight hours.

It was a rough night.

They kept me in what I termed the 'really sick' room in the ER. I had a nurse at my head and an intern or a physician at each one of my extremities. They kept asking me questions, but I couldn't talk to answer any of them. Finally, the nurse realized that my blood pressure had become elevated, and she surmised that I was struggling too hard to answer all the questions. They would have to find other ways to get their information.

I was admitted to the hospital very early that Wednesday morning. It was determined that I had suffered a stroke in a particular area of my brain stem that they could pinpoint. I would be in the hospital for three weeks before I would be able to return home.

What was I doing having a stroke, a twenty-nine-year-old woman who was healthy and active? For the first several days I was so exhausted, I simply couldn't process it. Although I was having a life-threatening experience there was never a moment where I felt I might not recover. That's one of the funny things about being a therapist. All my friends were therapists, so everyone who visited or called me was focused on my recovery.

The first ten days were the absolute worst. I was on

total bed rest which meant that I could not get out of bed for any reason. On day eleven I began some light physical therapy. I needed to build my strength back up to where I could take care of myself. My right arm and hand were weakened so I spent most of the time working to build back strength in my fingers and hand. Thankfully my speech was clear, but a little slow. While I couldn't talk for extended periods of time, I could at least be understood. About the third week I started in on my fine motor skills by working with big, fat crayons and coloring, working to more complicated tasks.

When I was released I went to my parent's house. I couldn't drive so they helped me through another three weeks of physical therapy. After that I finally got home and slept in my own bed for the first time in five weeks. Two weeks after that I returned to work. I worked part time for a couple of months and then back to my normal routine. By that winter, I was working again on my dissertation, which I completed and presented fourteen months later.

Today it has no day-to-day significance for me physically, but there are times when I know what happened. Sometimes I am very conscious of my balance when I am walking down stairs. When I'm real tired I notice my speech may be off a little. When I took up tennis a few years ago I discovered that I have difficulty running backward while looking up for the ball simultaneously. I could rewire myself enough to be able to play some good tennis. I have found my illness hasn't stopped me from doing anything.

I was told to be careful about having children. There was some question whether that would even be possible. I have a lesion that blocks part of the blood supply to my brain. The doctors were concerned about how a pregnancy and labor would affect my condition. I overcame the odds. I have two beautiful children.

Nobody in his or her right mind would ever ask to go through something like I went through. In retrospect though, I wonder where we learn some of the things we learn about life without experiences that demand so much from us. Most of what I had assumed about people I now know simply isn't true. I had always believed people could do anything they set their mind on. Now I realize that people may possess real limitations, both emotionally and physically. For some people there may be things that they simply can and cannot do. I am much more aware of an individual's capabilities and what is reasonable to expect from them. Because of the functionality I lost during my stroke I'm able to appreciate that some people may live in such places for a long time.

Another thing I learned is that life changes in the blink of an eye. The magic of life is that it always gives more than it takes.

What is our hope?

Barb's story shows us the commitment of recovery. All of us recover from our experiences and build back our strength. It is only through commitment to ourselves and to our recovery that we do that. Recovery is a difficult task both emotionally and physically, but it is worth every painful step. We all will be faced with the unexpected in one form or another, but it is the commitment we make to our recovery that starts the path to healing. Not all of us will be faced with retraining the motor skills in our hands or regaining our speech pattern, but each of us will face the importance of making a commitment to recovery. It could be our commitment to a drug regimen, or an exercise routine, or another change in our lifestyle that is important to our recovery. These all require commitments that we make to keep ourselves healthy. It only takes one at a time to prove that we can do it. Barb taught me that.

. . . Rita

Lori's Story

Lori, 40, is a single, professional woman raising a daughter. She was diagnosed with dysthymia (a form of depression) in 1998.

I was like most single, career-oriented women in their mid-thirties. I had built a solid foundation for my life. Solid foundations take planning and I am an expert at planning and executing. I worked hard to prove myself professionally, built my skills and knowledge and moved up in the organizations where I worked. Outside of work, my friendships and my family were my other priorities and having fun with them filled up a lot of my time. There had been a couple of serious relationships too. My life didn't seem all that different from other career women I knew.

When it came time to evaluate my career plan, I decided to make a change in my path. I made the decision to leave an organization that I had been with for ten years to become a consultant. It seemed like a natural step for me. It was a good use of my skills and knowledge. The travel was a challenge. My home was in Chicago and I worked on the East Coast. I would commute back and forth, packing up my things every week.

It was a lifestyle that kept me on the go and thinking fast.

My weekends were a blur. I would fly home on Friday, catch up on sleep, put my personal life back in order, see my friends, and return to the airport in time to catch my flight on Monday morning.

It made for a busy existence.

After a year, my lifestyle gave me plenty of opportunities to evaluate whether I was heading in the direction I wanted. While I enjoyed so much about my life, I realized after awhile that I didn't especially enjoy being on the road so much or staying in hotel rooms night after night. Beyond that were decisions I needed to make in my personal life that left me wondering. Had I made the right choices? I found myself beginning to ask questions about what I was doing that didn't seem to offer up easy answers.

Somewhere, I began to realize that my life wasn't

turning out as I had planned. It seemed as though I had reached a plateau professionally that I couldn't see beyond. There I was, thirty-six years old, not married, and no children. Not confident about my future, I wasn't sure I was living the life that I had imagined.

I remember thinking that all I needed was a simple attitude adjustment. There was no reason to be unhappy. After all, I had a great job, I was financially secure, I had just sold a house and was buying a brand new condo in the city. Who wouldn't be satisfied with that?

It turned out I couldn't. Slowly, it was becoming obvious that nothing I did was enjoyable to me. I began to feel like my whole life was simply the charade of going through the motions.

I knew enough not to blame myself. I began to look for ways to climb out of my fog, or meet someone who could help me adjust my attitude. I tried a couple of counselors, but neither seemed to find the words of encouragement I was looking for.

Not long after, I was talking to my sister on the phone, and she asked me about how I was feeling. It was clear that others were noticing that something was wrong. I casually brushed her off, but her observations troubled me. After hanging up the phone, I started thinking about it more seriously. I traced through my recent behavior to see if my sister was on to something.

At work, I was having trouble focusing on any task. I would find myself going to the soda machine or finding any excuse to leave my office because I couldn't keep my focus. I would call my friends or family constantly to talk to make the day go by because I just didn't have the concentration to perform. On weekends I was constantly on the move. I would spend weekends at my friends' homes or visit my family. I realized that I was never home for any length of time by myself. What was all of this adding up to?

Later that day I pulled a co-worker aside. I asked him to spend a few minutes with me. I described my recent conversation with my sister and asked his opinion.

"What do you think?" I asked him. "Is it me that's insane, or is it my sister?"

I will never forget my co-worker's response.

He would not tell me that I was okay. I needed for him to tell me that everything was all right, but he wouldn't do it. He mumbled something noncommittal and excused himself.

That was the first time I really knew that something might be wrong.

The next day, a friend came to spend the weekend with me in New York. I managed to be the happy-go-lucky sightseer, but inside I was churning. I was showing something on the outside that wasn't real on the inside.

I was becoming more miserable than I could bear.

It's amazing how I felt looking at my life from a perspective such as that. Removed. Detached. Our hotel room was on a high floor above Manhattan, and I remember looking out the windows. Then I had the thoughts. They were just nanoseconds. But they were there. They were my first thoughts of suicide.

How did I get myself to this place in my life?

By Monday, I was clearly out of focus. I couldn't concentrate on anything for more than five minutes. I was getting very upset that I couldn't get anything done. I made an important decision to see a psychologist and called for an appointment that very day. I left work and flew home so that my sister could go with me. I knew this was something I didn't want to do alone. After some tests and a few counseling sessions, he sat down and explained everything to me.

"Lori," said the psychologist, "you have what is called dysthymia. It is a form of depression." He told me that my treatment plan would be a combination of counseling and medication and that it could take a year to eighteen months to stabilize me. That session was very hard for me. I'm grateful my sister was along, because I don't know whether I would have been able to comprehend everything my counselor was telling me.

I began treatment right away. I tried various

medications. It took two years of searching for a combination of medications and a dosing schedule that would work for me. It took that long to get me to a place where I could begin to function. Counseling is where the "real" work began. We started to break my life down into basic components. This allowed me to clearly identify my road to recovery. It would be important that I begin to isolate things in my life to appreciate.

I would need to choose to be happy and that would be a difficult thing for me to do. I also realized that this was not just a recent event for me. As I began to look at my life, I realized that I had been suffering from depression for years, maybe even decades. This was not just brought on by a stressful, dissatisfying time in my life. This had been present for as long as I could remember. My recovery would require me to rebuild my whole emotional structure in order to function like everyone else.

I already felt as though I was carrying more baggage than I could bear. Now I had the label of a mental illness as well. I found out that others in my family's past had battled the same disease. No one had ever talked about it. It was hard not to be angry about being kept in the dark. I knew that someone would have to break the code of silence about the illness. I felt that it was my job to educate other family members. I would need to step up and share what was happening to me with my loved ones.

I made the decision to return to work during the first days of my recovery, but it didn't go smoothly. The medication wasn't helping me, so I decided to take two months away for myself. It was important that I took the time away because I was finding that the smallest things overwhelmed me. At times, it was a struggle to make the trip to the grocery store to buy a loaf of bread. Sometimes any decision, no matter how small, seemed insurmountable. There were some days when I found it difficult to even get out of bed. In every way, I felt exhausted and alone.

I don't know what I would have done if loving people hadn't surrounded me. I found it hard to ask for help, but once I did I found true generosity. At one point loved ones paid my bills, bought my groceries, and did about everything one could imagine in helping me stay functional. Since this wasn't something that many people around me were aware of, those closest to me became my life support. My family and close friends formed a circle of protection for me that kept me insulated and safe. Whether it was running errands for me, staying with me or sometimes just watching television so I wouldn't be alone, they always made me feel insulated, safe and let me know that they cared about me. They allowed me to stay focused on my counseling sessions and find my way through my recovery.

After a couple of months, I began to notice a difference. I went back to work and began a steady period of recovery that lasted about three years. It was after that three-year period of counseling and medication that I felt I was functioning well.

In looking back, it's amazing how much raw effort my recovery required of me. It wasn't like I was sitting around in bed waiting for my body to heal itself. I was required to invest every bit of myself - mentally and emotionally - to the healing process. During that time, I would have nanoseconds of positive feelings. I had never experienced those before in my life. My counselor helped me focus on these as a part of my recovery. Our job in counseling was to "lengthen" those feelings and experiences for me – to find those positive experiences and make them last longer and longer. It also helped tremendously once we could isolate the proper medication. Then my progress accelerated.

Today I am in a healthy place. I am at last content with my life and what my future looks like. While my life may not turn out quite like I had imagined it is to be treasured nonetheless. It's important for me to stay focused on the day at hand and react accordingly.

The boundaries that I set for myself protect me from

expectations that may be impossible for me or others to meet. I have learned that although schedules and plans are important to me, it's okay to modify these plans and work through changes as they come.

I never could have anticipated how critical my counselor would be to my recovery. In the face of a disease like this, I could always tell my counselor what I was feeling without having to worry about value statements coming back at me. It was a safe place for me to learn about the person that I was and teach myself about the person that I wanted to be. I learned to rely on my counselor for truth and direction regarding my future. He helped me see the people around me in a more realistic light. It became important to have a safe place to just be, a place where I could begin to reassemble my pieces.

I learned how to hope. I take care of myself now. I put myself first. I am tapping into a more emotional side of my personality. Knowing what I have been through, I am more tolerant of people and less judgmental. I used to react to situations with learned behavior and habit. Now I make clear choices in my life. My choices. When you are struggling against something that could defeat you, it is important to be able to see the light and way out. I found that light. For me, hope is perseverance.

What is our hope?

Lori's story takes courage to tell and to read. Lori is one of my best friends and has taught me more about support and courage than anyone. There are millions of people who face depression every day in our society. It can be functionally disabling, and if gone unnoticed, undiagnosed or untreated, it can threaten the lives of our family members, friends, and neighbors. We need to continue to break through the myth that depression is about "attitude adjustments" as Lori says in her story. Watching someone you care about suffer from depression can leave you feeling just as helpless and saddened as watching someone struggle with any of the other diseases portrayed in this book. While Lori's story is only one woman's view of the disease, it is my hope that we can continue to shed light on the significance of depression, how it can affect any one of us, and more importantly, how it can be treated through counseling and the use of medications.

. . . Rita

Sarah's Story

Sarah, 36, is a single, urban professional. In 1993, she was diagnosed with multiple sclerosis (MS).

My story begins a long time ago, back in 1993.

I was twenty years old and a junior at Rutgers University. I don't know if you can remember exactly how it feels to be that young, energetic and alive, but I sure can. Days didn't have enough hours in them for me. I rode my bicycle everyday and played lots of tennis with my friends.

I was very active, and I wouldn't have had it any other way.

I was in the middle of a full load at Rutgers University, which was as challenging as it sounds. I had my own apartment and after a lot of hard work, I was just two semesters away from graduating with a degree in communications. I loved challenging myself intellectually and physically.

Everything seemed to be falling right in line for me. I don't believe I had realized any sense of personal limits yet. Anything I wanted to do, I simply did.

During that particular winter, I was home visiting my parents one weekend and noticed something odd. While I was shaving my right leg, I realized that I couldn't feel the razor on my shin like I normally could. That caught my attention, but I thought it was related to some trouble I previously had with my sciatic nerve from running track in high school. Nevertheless, as a precaution I made an appointment to see an orthopedic surgeon just in case. They ran some tests, but they couldn't come up with anything out of the ordinary. I was given some anti-inflammatory medications and sent home to get better.

The "get better" part didn't happen.

It wasn't long before the sensation was spreading upwards into my groin area. I went to see my internist. She did some blood draws to check for Lyme disease, which was prevalent in Central New Jersey, especially at that time. All my tests kept coming back negative.

At that point, I was referred to a neurologist who did peripheral nerve tests to see whether I had injured myself somehow. That was followed by some more blood draws, MRIs of my spine and brain, and a spinal tap. The first thing that showed up on the radar screen was my white blood cell count. When it came back extremely high, my doctor began to mention the possibility of MS, or multiple sclerosis.

My father used the MS Society to find a neurologist who specialized in MS and before long, it was confirmed. I indeed had multiple sclerosis.

By the time I was officially diagnosed, I had become used to hearing those words. I remember the first time my internist suggested it as a possibility, and it felt as though someone had kicked me in the stomach. I was not expecting to hear that kind of news! When an MS specialist confirmed my diagnosis, my feelings were more fear, concern and frustration. My doctor encouraged me to ask questions, and I found that the more I asked, the better I began to feel. He gave me hope. He told me that it appeared that I had a mild form of the disease. I was concerned about ending up in a wheelchair, and he told me that less than 25 percent of MS patients ended up that way. The more he talked, the more I realized that there were more facts than I could retain in my head. Just when

I thought I had digested one item, I needed to think fast to make room for another one.

I began to make regular trips to the library and started to read everything I could get my hands on about my disease. I found that most of what I was discovering, I could keep straight by putting it into mental compartments. It wasn't long before I began to understand what was really happening to me.

The emotional side wasn't as easy to manage. Every emotional adjective you can write down described what was going on within me. I was confused, terrified, sad, mad and surprised — all simultaneously. It was difficult to take in all that was happening to me, and the emotions seemed to go in cycles. Just when I thought I had battled through all the emotions and was emerging on the other side, the cycle started over again. I never knew how long I would have between cycles — it could be a month, or it could be a year. I finally realized that all I could do was let my mind steer me through the emotional downswings whenever they would occur. I could "think" my way through it. I could turn to my mind for help.

Of all the adjustments MS has forced upon me, the most challenging has been the need to rethink what was truly possible for me. I know it sounds cliché, but I don't know how someone could appreciate how I think about myself unless they have had to make room in their thinking for a disease like I have. In some ways, I feel trapped. My body doesn't serve me in the way it once did. My memory and focus are significantly different. Sometimes I can't walk a block or two anymore without someone lending me their hand. This kind of vulnerability makes me feel less confident.

I believe, for me, I am reaching the most difficult part of my disease. During the early days, it felt like what was happening to me was largely dependent on my personal efforts to battle my way out. If I would make the time to work out, I could feel the difference in my body, and I felt as though I was winning. Even when I would feel the pins and needles and all the weird sensations that accompanied MS, I would put them aside, thinking that they were passing and soon to be gone. The drugs I was on usually returned me to a degree of normalcy, and I had a sense of ease in getting over my attacks and moving forward. It was all very manageable.

Today, I have to rebuild everything about myself. I have to change the way I think about who I am and what I can do. Life now has very definite limits. There are things I can do and lots of things that I cannot. I live in a large city, so walking up and down subway stairs finds me noticing how awkward my left leg moves from step to step. I take pains not to trip. I am sometimes so focused on the immediate "next step" that sounds and noises easily startle me. I have to re-establish things I can do for myself, so that I can begin to have confidence in myself again. Since so much of MS takes a physical toll, I find I need to replace its effects with personal intellectual achievements. Once again, I am turning to my mind for enrichment where my body has limits. It's a journey that never ends.

Luckily for me, I received much of what I needed along the way to keep myself in a healthy place. I have always received the best treatment whenever I needed it, as fast as I could get it. My family has always surrounded me and constantly filled me with their never ending love and support. It doesn't matter what I need, where I am or what time it is, they are always there. There are also friends, mentors and great doctors encouraging me every step of the way. I continue to find it easier to win when I am winning as a team.

Ten years after my diagnosis, I am a different person in so many ways. Physically, the changes that I face daily are my greatest challenge. I am weaker in my left arm, left leg, and left hip. Functioning in a large city can be quite a challenge with busy streets and lots of traffic and constant noises. I have to pay attention daily to how my new limitations may affect the way I move through and plan my day.

Ten years is a long time. In traveling this path, my body may be less resilient but I am intellectually and spiritually stronger than ever. I appreciate life more than I ever have, and the gift of health has become the greatest treasure of all. Over time I think I have managed to figure my disease out, and I have made room for it in my life.

What is our hope?

Sarah paints us a portrait of living with a disease for which there is no cure. Facing a diagnosis initially is a painful experience for all of us. Learning to navigate through the ever-changing demands of her illness and continually restore herself is a message that we all can take with us from this story. Sarah has taught us through her story to accept the emotional cycles that come with living with a condition such as MS. She also has helped to show us that we can see our way through these cycles to a healthier place. Living with a chronic disease is not easy, by any stretch of the imagination. Through Sarah's eyes, we see that we can discover how to enrich our lives in new and different ways. These new pursuits may bring opportunities and dreams that once again make our lives seem without limits.

. . . Rita

Reneé's Story

*Reneé, 46, is a divorced,
professional woman with one
daughter. In 1994, she was
diagnosed with breast cancer.*

So my claim to fame is that my body got attacked. I'm not sure that is exactly how I want to be remembered, but now I'm stuck with the story.

It seemed like for much of my life everything seemed rather ordinary. I had worked my way into a fairly basic life. I married, had a job and was a mother with a teenage daughter. I had all the school functions scribbled on my calendar, made dinner most every night and I kept myself pretty busy. Most everything seemed to be in the right place.

I don't remember the very day I felt the pain for the first time, but I do remember that the pain didn't want to go away. It started as an ache in my left armpit. It got so bad that I started having difficulty lifting my left arm. I thought for sure that I had injured myself doing yard work or something around the house. Even the doctor thought I had strained something, so he gave me some painkillers and told me to come back in a month if the pain didn't go away.

It didn't go away.

I was back the following month, so the doctor suggested we do a baseline mammogram. I wasn't surprised when the mammogram came back clean, so I left the doctor's office with a prescription for some muscle relaxants and the peace of mind that the pain should work itself out.

But it wouldn't go away.

I returned the following month, and we repeated the mammogram. It came back clean a second time, but this time the doctor wasn't satisfied.

"I want to do a biopsy," he told me.

"A biopsy? Do you really think we need to?" I asked.

"I want to be safe," he said firmly. "You aren't getting any better, and since it's more toward your chest wall, I want to make sure we aren't missing anything."

I stopped by the front desk on the way out and

scheduled myself for the biopsy. I remember walking out to the car and wondering what the doctor thought he would find. In three months of visits, the word cancer had never come up, not even once. The "C" word was the furthest thing from my mind.

The morning of the biopsy is still a bit of a blur. When I woke up, someone told me that it was cancer. I was sure it couldn't be me she was talking about. She had to have confused me with someone else.

"Are you sure you are looking at the right results?" I asked my doctor when he came in to see me.

He shook his head. "I want you to see a surgeon right away," he said.

I'm sure there was a lot of talking that went on after that, but I don't remember a single word of it. My mind never got around the surgeon part. I would see a surgeon. Why would I need to see a surgeon? I didn't have cancer. This was all messed up.

My friend Deb from work came in to take me home. She was crying, and rubbing my back and telling me that I would get through this. I couldn't understand what she was crying about. I was fine. There wasn't anything wrong with me.

When I got home, another friend, Laura, was in the house waiting for me. I think my husband called her and asked her to meet me there.

"This is not a death sentence," she said teary-eyed when I arrived. "We can beat this. We will fix you."

The rest of the day is gone from my memory. I have no recollection of anything else that was said or who I talked with. I don't even remember telling my daughter when she got home from school. I took a Vicodin® and went to bed. I would wake up in the morning, and everyone would see that they had made a mistake. Thirty-five-year-old women didn't get breast cancer. I just needed to sleep.

I woke up the next morning, but I had problems waiting for me. My three-inch long incision had broken open, and I was covered in blood and discharge. I remember that was the first moment that it hit me something was wrong. I don't mean wrong because the stitches had broken open. I mean that something was seriously wrong with my body.

And I knew at that moment that I had cancer.

I called Laura, and she rushed over to patch up my incision. Then we got on the phone to make my next appointment. I needed to see a surgeon right away.

By the time I sat down for my consultation, I felt that I was on the front of a runaway freight train.

"I recommend you consider a mastectomy. If we are lucky, we can get you another five to ten years," he said.

Have you ever sat in a chair and looked totally

stupid? I mean like completely stupid because you have no frame of reference for the words you are hearing? I was sitting across from the surgeon and struggling to make sense of the gibberish I was hearing.

Five to ten years? A mastectomy and then I only get five to ten years?

Yesterday, I was fine. How was this happening? I had a little girl who needed me. I was too young to die in five or ten years.

For the rest of the week I stayed in a very dark place. I felt as though I had been given a death sentence. Someone had reached down from heaven and grabbed my chart and pronounced "Okay, let's stop this right now. We aren't taking this life any further."

I had cancer.

And it was threatening to take away my life.

Wow.

I had no experience in this. I felt like the characters in the movies. Maybe I should quit my job and spend my last days with my daughter. What difference would it make? Nothing mattered anymore, anyway.

I stayed in what felt like an emotional darkness for days. Then one morning, I woke up and sat on the edge of my bed talking to myself.

"Well," I whispered, " I have a choice to make. I can lie around here and be defeated. But I have never given up before. I have always managed to come out on top. I have a little girl. I need to find the best doctors and do whatever I need to do to survive because I need to be a part of my daughter's life."

I stood up and realized that I had made a decision to fight my cancer. "I will not let this get me down," I said, gritting my teeth.

When I went back to work, word had spread fast about my diagnosis. Right away two women called me and told me how they had beaten their cancer. As they talked to me, I knew that I could beat this thing. If they could do it, I could do it. They were like a breath of fresh air.

I had been told that my cancer was like a dandelion, so the challenge was to remove it all so it wouldn't grow back. My doctor was patient and spent every minute that I needed to walk me through all of my options, whether we would elect for a lumpectomy or a mastectomy. He asked me to go home and sleep on my decision.

I went home, but I couldn't sleep. All I could think about was getting this thing out of my body. I weighed the option of saving my breast and having the lumpectomy. But I knew, deep down, I couldn't walk around wondering, "Did we get it all?" I could not live that way.

On the day of the surgery, the surgeon performed a mastectomy and removed twenty-eight lymph nodes that would need to be tested. Two proved to be cancerous.

The surgery was a success.

After I recovered from my surgery, it was on to the next step. It wasn't long after the surgery that I was headed to my next course of treatment-chemotherapy, twice a month for six months. Slowly but surely, we were winning the battle.

I was on my way back.

I know it's usual for women to say how different they are after going through something like this, but it's really true. I was faced with choices that I never thought I would have to make. I had to take control of my life and my health at a time when I never expected I would have to think about it. I had to learn how to truly take care of myself.

Right now, I am enjoying my eighth year of remission and I am at peace with my body. The cancer may be gone from my body, but it will never be gone from my mind. Each day it moves a little farther behind me. In a way, the experience will never leave me because of what it has taught me about myself. It has made me stronger and taught me how to cherish others and myself.

You know, it's nice not to have to be "super" any more. You know, Supermom, Superwife, Superemployee, Superhousekeeper . . . I realize that no one ever really had that expectation, except me. I only have to be me. For one more day. I have found that makes everybody who loves me very happy.

What is our hope?

Reneé's story explores one woman's emotional struggle in facing a disease and making critical choices. The amount of information thrust upon us in a short amount of time is overwhelming as we sit in our doctor's offices wishing we were anywhere else. Everyone feels overwhelmed in these situations. It is important to take the time we need to make the decisions we feel are right for our bodies and ourselves. There must be time for asking questions and understanding our options. While we may not have weeks or months, it is still important to take whatever time we are given to feel comfortable with our choices. We are the only ones who have to live in our skin and feel comfortable with the decisions that we make about our own health. Reneé taught me that understanding your choices is the most important part of accepting what comes next in your path. As my sister, she plays an important role in my life, but she also plays an important role in my health by sharing her story with me and being an important connection for me when I was trying to learn how to make choices for myself.

                                                    . . . Rita

Vicki's Story

Vicki, 44, is married and is raising one son. In 1994, she was diagnosed with scleroderma and polymyositis.

I am no stranger to the challenges of life. I watched my mother struggle with lupus for years. She eventually died from kidney failure in 1993.

I guess you could say that during the time I cared for her, I developed a rather predictable routine. I think it's one of the ways I managed to survive. I worked from five in the morning to noon, seven days a week. I would finish work as a bookkeeper at a local restaurant, go home, let my dog out, and then go to my mother's house, make her lunch, pick up my son from school, go back and make dinner, and then go home to get ready for the next day.

It was my life until my mom died. I guess it was okay because I love to take care of people. My son and I took care of each other and together we took care of my mother. The three of us were a close-knit family until 1993, when my mother passed away.

In 1994, I noticed some unusual things beginning to happen with my body. My face and my hands got all puffy, and my doctor confessed to being mystified as to the cause. He sent me to a rheumatologist, and suggested that he take a look. At first, my symptoms seemed to mimic so many other diseases, which made it a challenge to diagnose. I changed physicians, and on my very first visit, the new doctor finished my blood work and rolled up on the stool next to me.

"Well, that's not too much of a mystery," he said. "It looks like you have what your sister has." That would mean scleroderma and polymyositis.

My sister had been diagnosed with scleroderma and polymyositis five years earlier. Since we weren't very close, I hadn't been involved in her disease.

Now, I was stunned.

Scleroderma is a connective tissue disorder that causes the skin to get rigidly tight and thick. For some reason, I couldn't imagine that I had the same disease as my sister. My thoughts blurred. I remember not knowing how to react and not knowing where to go for support. I wouldn't have much time for confusion.

Often times the disease affects the major organs as well. Usually the heart is one of the last organs to feel its effects. It took just weeks for it to affect mine.

Three weeks after my diagnosis, I wasn't feeling right. Since I had just started a high dose of prednisone, which is an oral steroid, I thought perhaps it was a reaction to the medication. I called the doctor and it turned out it wasn't the medicine, but my disease reaching deeper into my body—right for my heart. My doctor told me to go straight to the hospital. I remember crying as I packed my suitcase. By that evening, I was in cardiac care. The tests showed I had suffered a heart attack. I was in the hospital for ten days.

When I got out, I began to face the daily realities of my disease. It wasn't long before the skin on my body got tighter and tighter. The doctor would give me a gown to put on during my visits, and I couldn't get my arms behind my head to put it on because my skin had gotten so thick and tight. I couldn't open a can of pop because my skin wouldn't bend.

I was becoming a prisoner in my own body.

At that time, not many people had seen my condition before. Even for health-care professionals, it was a bit of an oddity. It wasn't unusual for a doctor to call in an associate to see what scleroderma looked like when I was in the office. I was becoming a poster child for my disease.

Before long I was taking so many drugs at such high doses that my personality and my appearance began to change. The pain was a bit of a problem, so I moved up to 30 milligrams or more of prednisone a day. Of course, that made my life even more challenging because while prednisone worked well at taking away my pain, a complicating side effect was an insatiable appetite for food. I ballooned from 145 pounds to 260 pounds.

It was ironic that of everything associated with my disease, my weight gain may have been the most difficult to deal with. I worked as a bookkeeper in a local restaurant where, just like the show "Cheers," everybody knew my name. I can remember hiding in the back room because I was embarrassed that people would see me looking like I did.

In 1994, a local newspaper published an article on scleroderma and I was featured in it. In the small town where I live, any publicity is a lot of publicity. I had wanted to keep a low profile, when suddenly I found my picture plastered right smack in the middle of the article. I was overweight, and my swollen face had tight skin and wrinkles around my eyes. Think about how you feel when you get your film developed and you aren't happy because a particular photo is not flattering to your appearance. Now imagine a picture a dozen times worse and seeing it published in your hometown newspaper.

But that incident became an important moment for my disease and me. In the article, scleroderma had been described as a disfiguring disease primarily affecting women. It had said that women were embarrassed to be seen in public with some of the disfigurements caused by the illness. When the newspaper printed the article, I became scleroderma to many people in my town.

After the newspaper ran its story, two women found me that had recently been diagnosed with the disease. I met one of them through a friend and the other at the restaurant. These people became important to me because they allowed me to provide encouragement to them. We created a circle of hope for each other.

My doctors kept pushing the envelope with my treatments. It had been almost five years since my diagnosis. One day I was sitting in the doctor's office and he leaned over and said, "Vicki, I don't think your skin feels as tight. What do you think?" He was right.

I had gone into remission. The worst was behind me.

That was two years ago.

It's funny what happens to you along the way when

you're busy wrestling with a disease. I still can feel the echoes of the beast—an occasional heartburn that drops me to my knees, a few fingers that are still bent, and some wrinkles around my mouth. But that's okay. I like these gentle reminders because they constantly whisper to me not to take my life for granted.

I think the biggest surprise has been the affect of my recovery on those close to me. My husband had loved me all the way through my disease—fat, thin, soft, and thick. But as I got better, he found it difficult to love me healthy. The same was true for a few of my friends. For some reason, they had trouble accepting my recovery. When I got better and it became time to celebrate, some of the people I had expected to be around me disappeared, including my husband. My marriage fell apart. To this day, it is one of the great mysteries of my illness.

Mysteries and miracles come with any disease, large or small. I am lucky to have found more miracles than mysteries. There is little doubt that my experience has made me a better person. It has helped me become more sympathetic and empathetic. I now find it easier to be patient with people and tolerant of differences that may exist, whatever they may be.

My son, who has shared so much of my life with me and has always been there for me, is now studying to become a doctor. And I have found a man who loves me for what I have become. He is now my husband, and he brings a new sense of family to my life.

Miracles can happen on so many different levels.

Who would have thought that a couple of them would weave their way to me?

What is our hope?

Vicki's story is a courageous one. She faced her disease with grace, perseverance and faith. The years that she continued the treatments that changed her appearance and personality might be more than some of us could bear, but Vicki is more brave than most. She never lost faith in herself and even became an example for her community and others with this disease. Women like Vicki make us all stronger through their willingness to be seen and heard.

. . . Rita

Kathy's Story

Kathy, 50, is a single, professional woman with two grown children. In 2000, she was diagnosed with Crohn's disease.

I was one of those rare people that you meet who enjoys her work. I had recently taken a job in the corporate sector of retail after coming out of a food brokerage background. Since my work has always been important to me, I was thinking about what might be next for my life. Even after taking the retail job, I was considering moving into a role where I could be more involved in doing what I loved to do most—helping people.

My life had always been a nonstop express. After a busy day of work, I would usually spend my evenings doing housework or going out to dinner with my friends. I had discovered how enjoyable it was to develop relationships around the experience of dining out, so it became one of my favorite pastimes. It is amazing what I could discover about people by the types of food they enjoyed and how they felt about what they ate. It's also the time you can have with people that seemed to be without boundaries or limits. I loved going out to restaurants with my friends.

Of course, that was before my life changed inside the blink of an eye. One week I was fine, and the next week I wasn't. One morning in May 2000 I noticed a cold sore in my mouth, which didn't seem so unusual. What was unusual was that by the end of the week I had seven. I made an appointment to see a doctor, trying to understand what could be causing my problem. Over the next two weeks I visited with several doctors, all of them trying to figure out what was happening to me. I was told to stay at home until I could get an appointment with an infectious disease specialist. Nobody was sure what was wrong with me.

Within that two-week period I couldn't keep any food down, and I was starting to lose weight. By the time I got in to see the infectious disease specialist, he didn't even want to touch me because of all the sores on the outside of my body.

"Have you been out of the country?" the specialist asked me. "Have you eaten any strange foods? Have you been living under unsanitary conditions?"

I answered negative to every question. Even the dermatologist wouldn't touch me. Nobody seemed to know what was affecting me, and people were afraid of getting too close.

I was getting scared—and concerned. What do you mean you don't know what this is? I thought. Then I would calm myself and think, they are saying that because they haven't explored everything yet. And I was right. We still had some exploration left to do.

Finally, the doctors told me they needed me in the hospital so they could get to the root of my problem. I had to wait a few days because the hospital was full, which gave me time to get real scared. On a Friday morning I checked in, and the parade of interns began.

It wasn't long before the implications of my medical history began to guide the investigation. My brother had battled Crohn's disease, and the talk among the doctors was that I might be suffering from the same condition. After two days in the hospital they started me on prednisone, an oral steroid to help my aching legs.

The disease was quickly proving to be relentless. I

had developed external sores, or ulcers, on the backs of my legs and all over my body. There was a cluster of sores that had broken out behind one of my knees that made it almost impossible for me to walk normally. The sores made my skin feel like I had the worst sort of sunburn, so clothes were not comfortable to wear at all. So that made it difficult for me to function in my everyday life for a while.

Then it was confirmed: I was told that I had Crohn's disease.

The next step was to determine whether it had spread into my colon. That was the first moment I felt myself losing a grip on what was happening. I had watched my brother struggle with this disease for twenty years before it spread into his colon and caused his early death. I remembered that he only had a sore or two on his legs all that time and here I had them all over my body, including the bottoms of my feet and on my scalp. I found myself wondering how long I would be in pain before I died. I was deathly afraid.

The tests came back negative, so my colon was safe for the moment. It was primarily in my small intestines, so I would have to immediately modify my diet. I was told my case hadn't reached a critical phase yet.

The mental adjustment I faced was daunting. Crohn's disease flares up whenever it has a mind to.

Sometimes the flare-ups are referred to as "social embarrassments" because you have no control. I thought to myself, how am I going to work? I was wondering how long a company would put up with an unpredictable employee. Would they let me go? How would I support myself as a single person?

I was placed on Remicade® (infliximab) and anti-inflammatory drugs. By the third day, I started to feel better. My diet consisted of clear liquids and pureed foods. By Tuesday, I was allowed to go home, five days after I had checked in.

For some reason, I tried returning to work two days later. I must have looked awful. I was down to 90 pounds, and I felt very weak. I remember looking at all my pills on the counter that morning, thinking, I have become like my father, taking fifteen pills a day. My father had Parkinson's disease, and he had been on a rigid schedule of medication for some time.

During those early days, the permanency of my condition hadn't sunk in. I thought that maybe I would take the medication for six months, and then I wouldn't need it anymore. I thought if I did all the right things, I would be fine. That became my goal.

After a couple of visits to my doctor I realized that my plan would never happen. I would have to keep taking my medication for a long time. I began to question what effect taking drugs would have on my body. I had seen my brother watch his medication become less and less effective over the years, and I wondered how much time I had before the same thing happened to me.

I had to rethink my love affair with dining out. Food no longer offered the same romance that it once had. Seemingly overnight, most of my favorite foods were off-limits to me. One of my favorites, raw vegetables was suddenly a major no-no. I remember thinking that if everything cleared up, and I could get myself off the medication, then maybe I could eat vegetables. I was in denial. It wouldn't happen.

Several months later, in November, I attended a seminar for Crohn's patients. It felt like a good thing to do. I thought it would be a good opportunity to gather all kinds of information and ask all kinds of questions. Instead, I left feeling very alone and depressed. Every other person who attended came with a family member or a friend. I had gone by myself. It made me realize that I was trying to cope with a major event in my life all alone.

I walked away from the seminar with a few realizations. I understood that no matter how good I was with my medications and diet, this disease was still going to flare up whenever it wanted. I realized that this would be the lifestyle I would have forever. I also realized that this was the body that I would have for as long as I was here. I needed to accept that.

I felt the need to share everything I was learning with my sons and brother, since Crohn's disease is hereditary. This process became part of my emotional healing. I hadn't had anyone in my life to share the emotional side of my struggle with on a daily basis. So I discovered that sharing the information with family members became a way for me to cope with my disease. I could help myself by educating those around me.

My roommate brought a great sense of emotional support for me, and I don't know what I would have done without her. My food menus, especially during the first year, were so limited that I think I would have starved without her. I could have no skins, no fruits, no wheat, no seeds (which means, not many fast food choices), no fatty foods, and no beans. I might have three tablespoons of fish or chicken with some noodles for a meal. I usually ate some cereal for breakfast. The encouragement I received from my roommate helped me through some really discouraging times. There were many times when I couldn't believe I was the same woman who would eat out one or two nights of the week. I really missed my Taco Bell Wednesdays.

One of the toughest aspects of having a disease like this is when one has to take it on alone. I have to be conscious of my spending because part of my financial responsibility is to keep myself healthy with medications. The financial burden of my disease is always in the back of my mind. Early on, I felt the emotional drain of not having someone to stand alongside me. I think even a "buddy" to go through it with me would be a big help— someone to be there with me at doctor appointments and help me understand what I was going through. My friends and family were there for me after my appointments when I needed someone to talk to, but I needed someone by my side.

Today I still find one of my greatest outlets is educating others about my disease. It seems that the more I talk about Crohn's, the more I understand it. Letting people know also helps me define how I feel about my disease, and that makes it real for me. That's what makes it sink in. It helps me cope.

Life certainly looks different from the inside of a disease like this. I see my life as a whole now. I realize that my body is not my own, that I am just passing through. I will have a new body waiting for me someday. I feel strongly that we are the clay and that the Lord is our potter. He began a good work in me and will carry it to completion. I realize that I may not be the healthiest person, but I am still healthier than many people. I can stand beside them and help them through a difficult time. Where my body may not be what it once was, my faith has grown stronger and is sustaining me.

I also have discovered just how fragile life is and how fragile I am. My kids tell me I am a tough bird, but I know the truth of the matter. I think about how each day is more important than the last, and I try to live each day just that way.

What is our hope?

Kathy's story brings a sense of hope and spirituality. All of us who have faced an illness look for our sense of "control" in our situations. Understanding and accepting that even if we follow all the steps and do everything we are supposed to do in our therapy, we may still have obstacles to overcome. This is an important realization when you are dealing with a disease that can be unpredictable, such as Crohn's disease. Crohn's disease can be an extremely difficult disease for patients to manage and will certainly test the limits of a patient's will. Kathy has shown us that while her body may provide her with challenges, her spirit has never been stronger. There is a higher power from which we can all draw strength when we need it, and I want to thank Kathy for reminding us of that. I think it is important to learn that we can always replace our sense of control with a sense of faith.

. . . Rita

Rita's Story

Rita is 30 years old and is
engaged. She has been living with
cystic fibrosis since birth and also
has Type I Diabetes. In 2002, she
underwent an amputation of her
lower leg.

A life less ordinary . . . that's what I have. I don't
think of myself as extraordinary. I just make it
through each day, one day at a time. I spend time
with my family and my friends. I go to church. I
work on growing my relationship with my fiancé.
It may be ordinary by some people's standards, but
for me, it's special.

As 2002 began, I was working part time. Like many other people, I became a victim of corporate down-sizing and a weakened economy. My position was eliminated. I was in the midst of planning a wedding so I looked at this as an opportunity. Planning a wedding can be a full time job. My fiancé and I had set the date for September of 2002. There was still much to be done before the big day. There were dresses to be chosen, invitations to be designed, cakes to be tasted and music to be heard.

The date was drawing closer. In mid July everything was going smoothly; all except for the problems I started having with my left leg. It occurred rather suddenly. One morning as I started to get out of bed, I noticed some pain in my left foot. As the days went by, the pain grew worse. I would wake up, lean out of bed and put my foot on the floor. It would immediately ache. The pain made it difficult for me to walk. It got to the point where I couldn't stand on my left foot. I started to use crutches. The pain in my ankle was excruciating. It was time to start looking for some answers.

I went to my doctor and they started running tests. From describing my symptoms, they thought my problem was vascular, in nature. They ran initial tests and discovered that all of the arteries in my calf were blocked. The circulation to my foot was basically 'cut off'. They determined that this was a complication of my diabetes. That was my diagnosis.

That is how everything really started.

This discovery pushed me into another series of tests - angiograms and other vascular related tests that would hopefully point to a solution to my dilemma. The first potential solution was to put a stent in my leg. Stents are mesh-like tubes that are inserted into blood vessels to restore or increase blood flow. The stent that was put in my leg did not improve my situation. The doctor had told me from the beginning that this could be the case. I was not prepared for what was to follow.

The doctors continued to prepare me for the worst case scenario. The arteries were small and the blockages were located very far down in my leg. They felt that bypass surgery may not be a successful option for me. After the results of the first angiogram, the doctors told me that amputation was a definite possibility. I just kept thinking, "Why would he be telling me this, there has to be something that they can do?" I kept searching for more options. There had to be another way.

At the beginning of August, I started to explore if there were any other paths for me to travel. I went to different research-based hospitals, including the

University of Chicago. While I was there being tested, they told me that they could try some surgical options to open up the arteries in my ankle. It was an aggressive strategy. Then the specialist explained the other side of the coin to me.

"If we perform this procedure and try to open up the arteries in your ankle and it is unsuccessful, we will have to amputate, right then and there," he said.

He said that they would not be able to determine my exact situation until they were 'in there'. He went on to say that the best course of action would be to admit me to the hospital and go forward with the procedure immediately. It was very aggressive. I really felt like I didn't have any choice at all. I needed to take the time; I just wasn't ready to make this decision.

I went to the Mayo Clinic. They ran the same tests and I heard the same news. The arteries were too small and bypass would not do anything to improve my situation. Amputation was turning out to be my only option. The doctors told me that I could wait and let them know when I was ready. I didn't know if I would ever be ready. I was scared and frustrated.

I went home and tried to function. In the meantime, my condition had gotten worse. I couldn't walk at all. I couldn't put any weight on my foot. I was at a point where I couldn't walk, so I just stayed in bed. After a while, I had to make a decision. I couldn't stand to be this way anymore. What was I going to do, stay in bed all the time? That wasn't a life for me. I had plans and a life to live. And that was it. I made the choice to go forward with the surgery.

My fiancé and I made the decision to postpone our wedding. While I was facing this difficult situation, he was always supportive and always there for me. This time was no different. Our wedding day will come and it will be a true celebration of our love and commitment to each other. In our lives, we celebrate that commitment every day already.

The date was set for the surgery. In a way, I felt a sense of relief after I made the choice. It was the most difficult choice that I would ever make, but now, at least there were no more questions or wondering about what would happen next. There was a clear path for me. I found some comfort in that. In November of 2002, I went into surgery and my leg was amputated just a few inches below the knee. I came through the surgery well.

My recovery from surgery took a little longer. Because of my diabetes, my incision took longer to heal. It was important that my healing was complete before I started with my next challenge. I was fitted and started to work with a prosthetic leg. To say the least, it was weird. But I was determined.

"I can't stay in bed anymore," I said. And that was that.

I started going to physical therapy twice a week. The physical therapy was to 'fit the leg' so it didn't hurt anywhere or put pressure on the wrong places. If it wasn't fitted properly, it could cause damage to my leg or my knee. It was important for me to learn how to walk with the prosthetic because this was now a part of my life. Once the fitting was complete and I started the physical therapy, the rest came pretty fast for me. I was walking unassisted in a short amount of time. My sessions were twice a week and now they are down to once a week.

My therapy has gone extremely well. It is important for me to walk as much as possible. It is the best way to build up my muscles and keep my circulation going. I hadn't used those muscles very much the few months prior to my surgery. Even though I am making great progress, it will take a bit longer. I'm not worried. I will get all of my strength back. I am walking now, under my own power and with my own strength.

I realized how important my own power, strength and independence were when I felt confined to my existence. There were times when I would get frustrated and upset. The independence that I sought felt elusive because of my condition. My family, friends and my fiancé were more supportive than I could have ever imagined throughout my life. They were attentive, giving and helped me through this with more faith and inspiration than I could have asked for, but every once in a while, I craved my own 'self'. I have gained my 'self' back from this experience.

This is another new beginning for me. I have my life back. I have regained my independence through the most difficult choice, which at times, felt like no choice at all. I am now going out with my friends again. I am starting to drive again and go more places. I am able to have a routine about my life. My fiancé and I are still building our life together and someday soon we will celebrate our wedding day.

What is our hope?

Rita shows us the meaning of strength and courage. Faced with similar choices, many of us may not have chosen to remain strong like Rita did. It may be hard to picture what courage looks like, but I can tell you, it is the story that you have just read. Rita is, for me, the ultimate example of strength and courage. She faced the most difficult choice imaginable. It may not seem like a choice, but there is always a choice. She came through with the same strength, resolve and ambition and followed her next path. My interview with Rita was a little over 3 months after her surgery. She shows us her incredible strength in her willingness to share her story with all of us. She is one of the more extraordinary people that I think I will ever encounter. We thank you Rita for your honesty, strength and courage.

. . . Rita

Ellen's Story

Ellen, 37, is a married, professional woman raising two children. In 1989, she was diagnosed with systemic lupus erythematosus (SLE).

Some blessings are found in places where you least expect them. When I was younger I worked part time at a hospital on the weekends, and took care of children in my home during the week so that I could be home with my son. I was active. I loved being outdoors, and enjoyed being with friends. I enjoyed life in those days, but now I have a life that I treasure.

If someone had told me when I was first diagnosed with Lupus that I would look back and actually feel more blessed today than I was before I was sick, I would not have believed them. But here I am. And I am happier, more balanced and more at peace than I have ever been.

In 1989, before my initial diagnosis, I considered my life to be normal. I was married and we had celebrated the birth of our first child. I enjoyed being outside and made frequent visits to the park with my son and the two small children I babysat. I was busy watching children all week and working as a cashier at the hospital on the weekends. At that time I was also pregnant with our second child and everything was going as planned. Everything seemed to be working out well for us.

Two weeks before the birth of my son in 1989, during a routine doctor's visit, I was told that there was a problem with my blood pressure. My blood pressure was very high and it concerned my doctor. At that stage of my pregnancy they weren't going to take any chances. The next thing I knew I was in the hospital and having an emergency cesarean section to deliver my second son. There were many possibilities for my rise in blood pressure. After the delivery and while I was still in the hospital the doctors took the opportunity to more thoroughly explore the causes behind what was going on. Before I was allowed to leave the hospital with my son a host of tests were run, including a bone marrow biopsy. There was concern that I might have leukemia. Thankfully, the test came back negative and I was allowed to go home. There were no real answers for me yet.

When I arrived home I wasn't prepared for the amount of fatigue I faced. Though I was still recovering from my son's delivery and now taking care of a newborn and my older son, this was a different kind of tired. Deep down tired. I started to notice other things too. My weight started to drop and in a short amount of time I had lost 30 pounds. I was having trouble with my hands. My fingertips began to hurt and at times they would go numb all together. I knew that this wasn't normal. I went to see my gynecologist and explained what was going on and that I wasn't feeling right.

"It sounds like you might have lupus", she said.

She referred me to a rheumatologist. First they thought I had leukemia and now it may be lupus. This didn't feel like a game of charades to me.

At that time, the rheumatologist's first course of action was to put me in the hospital to run a series of tests. I was in the hospital for a week. They performed a whole range of tests on me including blood work, an

EKG and even a kidney biopsy. I think he knew what he was looking for and just wanted to be sure. By the time I left the hospital we had definite answers. My gynecologist had been right. I had lupus.

It's not unusual for lupus to affect the internal organs. My kidneys were affected. In my case, my right kidney was more inflamed than my left. My rheumatologist prescribed prednisone, an oral steroid, to fight the inflammation. The side effects caught me a little by surprise. I started to put on weight, which I needed since I had recently lost so much. My face began to change and that was a little more difficult for me. Prednisone can give you a 'moon face' effect - bloating around your cheeks and chin. People who didn't know me or didn't know me well would look at me oddly because it was clear that someone looking like this wasn't normal. It made me feel uncomfortable and I lost some of my self-confidence. It was hard for me. I didn't want to feel like I needed to explain to the whole world that I had an illness and that is why I looked differently.

Lifestyle is very important in maintaining a healthy status with lupus. The doctor had warned me that stress would exacerbate my condition. I had to work hard to create an environment for myself that would lower my stress and create more balance in my life.

Easier said than done, but I had to try for my health. The other important factor was my diet. It was important for me to eat healthier. Healthy foods would help build up my immune system. I would work to try to build and maintain a low stress, healthy lifestyle. That lifestyle would be put to the test many times over the years.

My husband had always been a part of the Army reserves. In 1991, he went away for a four-month assignment. I had a hard time keeping it all together. Between taking care of the kids and having to focus on keeping myself healthy, I could feel the stress starting to build. It was so hard having him away. I started to see the changes in my body. It was reacting to the stress that I was under. My feet and ankles started to swell and I started to lose weight again. I was eating, but once again my weight started to drop. When my husband came home we went back to the rheumatologist.

The rheumatologist that had been treating me felt that it would be beneficial for me to start seeing a nephrologist. Since my disease clung to my kidneys and that's what nephrologists specialize in, kidney function, it was a perfect fit. My new doctor felt it was time to try a new set of treatments to battle my disease. Once a month I would go to the hospital for a weekend and receive these treatments through a catheter. When I got home each Sunday I was exhausted. I went through that process three times with no real success.

Then they tried chemotherapy. I received chemo twice a month. I was starting to spiral into depression. I had gone through the changes with taking the prednisone, but now my hair was falling out in clumps from the chemotherapy. My hair was falling out and I wasn't getting any better. Where was this all leading?

There was another woman that was at the hospital and people would get us confused sometimes. I was at the hospital a lot, between my treatments and working there part time on weekends. I was trying to keep up on her condition since she and I were similar and I felt like a kindred to her since people were always confusing us. I was at the hospital one day and I heard 'code blue'. The call was for her. She didn't make it. It was a turning point for me. I felt for her and I began to wonder when it would be my turn. I thought to myself, "I know I'm going to be next".

It was becoming scary for me. Nothing was working. My doctors were trying everything and my disease just wasn't responding. In 1993 I was back in the hospital. My platelets and hemoglobin levels were low. I needed a blood transfusion, followed six months later by a platelet transfusion to try and build up my immune system. That was a hard year. I was hospitalized three times.

Everyone chooses their own place to go and gain strength. There were times when I was so low I didn't know where I would get the energy to keep fighting. I knew I needed to talk to someone about how I was feeling. I chose my priest. He said some interesting words to me.

"Ellen", he said, "everyone will have their day. Only the Big Man will know when it's time for you. You have to live your life, taking it day by day, and live each day to its fullest".

Everyone has a turning point. That was mine. I listen and live by those words everyday. They comfort me when I am feeling down. Those words would provide me constant strength in the battle that was always ahead of me.

Through it all I continued to work part time on the weekends. But I had new, troubling symptoms. It was becoming hard for me to walk. When I stood I felt like there was a burden on me. I couldn't walk straight, and I began to fall frequently, especially on stairs. When I'd go to bed at night, my back would spasm.

With the new symptoms, came a new specialist. I was referred to a neurosurgeon who found that I now had hydrocephalus, which is excessive accumulation of fluid in the brain. Based on his knowledge, I was the second patient with lupus to be diagnosed with hydrocephalus. In 1994, I returned to the hospital for surgery. I needed a shunt to help drain the excess fluid from my brain.

It was difficult coming home after the surgery. Half my head had been shaved for the surgery, and I had staples from the surgery. My boys were small. They were afraid to come near me. That was so tough. My boys would look at Mommy differently for a while. But, even though it was hard I had so much support. My husband was wonderful. I relied on him. My friends and family rallied around me too. The people I needed most were there for me, and that made a big difference.

After the surgery and recovery my life began to stabilize. I got stronger and stronger. I felt myself beginning to build a sense of health, a sense of true recovery. After years of struggling I finally started to feel whole again. By the middle of 1994, five years after this ordeal had begun for me, I was beginning to go into remission. Living each day and concentrating on those words have proven to be the blessing that I was looking for after all. I have been in remission for eight years.

As with most of us, there are permanent changes that will be with me always. I will be on prednisone for the rest of my life. All of the medications have caused me to develop Type II diabetes. I now take about five to six pills a day to keep myself healthy. With everything that I have been through, taking daily medications, watching my blood sugar, and eating healthy is a small commitment to make and it is worth it.

Living my life became very deliberate for me as I emerged from my battles with my many diseases. I have learned to manage the stress level in my life and watch myself grow stronger and stronger with each passing day. I am very careful with my diet. I try not to let the little things bother me. I don't go out as much as I used to, instead I spend a lot of time with my husband and my sons. I concentrate on the things that are important to me. I work hard to reach out to others, to help them when they face trials, to shoulder their burden and help them find their way.

There is no doubt in my mind that I am a happier person now than I was before I was sick. After being concerned about matters of life and death, the small things that each day brings are appreciated as never before. While it has brought many changes, the core of life is there to be treasured and shared. And though I may never look the way I once did, that's okay. We come to accept these changes in our own time. Every day is a blessing to me and I want to live it to the fullest with those I love by my side.

What is our hope?

Ellen speaks with a quiet bravery and hopefulness. To meet Ellen is to meet a woman who has something to teach us about bravery and hope. Ellen's story is difficult because it takes us to a place where we don't dare go to face ourselves. Ellen brought to us honesty about what it feels like to stand on that edge and look back at yourself. The fear of facing death, so close that someone actually thinks it's you by confusing you with another woman in the hospital. The irony of the journey is not as important as what she discovered while she was there. Ellen brings us the gift of what she found; her true self, her faith and her strength to fight. Now she is sharing not only her story, but she shares her strength every day by working in the clinic where she was treated for her hydrocephalus. Thank you Ellen, because you are proof that there are angels among us.

. . . Rita

Kristin's Story

Kristin, 22, recently graduated from college. She was diagnosed with melanoma when she was 20 years old.

Everyone wants to make the most of their college experience. Enjoy everything, be a part of it all and I was no exception. I had worked hard to get here and I wasn't going to miss any opportunities. I was a sophomore at a Big Ten school, and it was all that it was cracked up to be. It was non-stop and I had the energy to do it.

My semesters were full. I don't think the word 'busy' would have covered my schedule during those months. I carried a full academic load, which is a feat in itself with a dual major. I was on the dance team, which meant hours of practice, four to five days a week. I was an officer in my sorority, so I spent a lot of time with my sorority sisters. Needless to say, time was a precious commodity in my world. I would also try to spend every other weekend with my boyfriend, who was at a different school. It was busy, but I loved it.

The summer of 1999 started like any other - that much needed break from school. It was time to relax. My boyfriend and I were doing just that one day in our bathing suits when he noticed the mole on my right side, just below my bikini top. Unfortunately, I couldn't really see it, but it was noticeable to other people with my bathing suit on. He suggested that I have it removed. I made an appointment with my internist to have it looked at first. Due to our insurance coverage, I needed the appropriate referrals. He told me it didn't look like anything to be concerned about and gave me the referral to the dermatologist. When I called to make the appointment for the dermatologist they were booked, and by that time I was already back in school.

School had ramped up for the semester and with my schedule and activities, it became low on the list of priorities. I didn't give it much thought. It wasn't until the next summer came and bathing suits were the attire of choice that I was reminded again of the mole. I went through the first round of referrals again as I was finishing the semester so I could be guaranteed an appointment with the dermatologist at the beginning of June.

Once again, the internist said, "It is sort of big, but it looks fine and should not be anything to worry about."

A couple of weeks later I was at my dermatology appointment to have the mole removed. As he was removing the mole he said, "Oh I'm 99% sure I will never see you again." That's how it all started, it was just a mole.

As is standard procedure, they sent the mole out to be tested. It took about two weeks to get the results back. I went on with my summer activities. That day began like any other summer day. My boyfriend and I were in my parent's driveway washing his car. My dad arrived, then my mom and my brother and his wife. I wasn't putting it all together at the time, but something was definitely going on. My mom asked me to come into the house. We went into the kitchen, sat down and she started to tell me the news.

"We got the results back and it was cancerous, you have melanoma", she said.

Wow! My thoughts were a bit jumbled at that moment. My dad had been treated for skin cancer. But this was different. I knew from his experience that there are different types of skin cancer. His was basal cell carcinoma which is a non-melanoma type of cancer, so I clearly understood the difference. His was more common and treatable. Mine was less common and a more aggressive type of cancer. This was serious. I believe my first question was "Am I going to die?" and my second question was "Am I going to lose my hair?" Clearly, I was in a lot of shock and a little out of focus, but five minutes ago, I was washing the car and now I had cancer.

My life came to a stand still for a little while. I wasn't sure what to think or what to feel. I was so thankful that my mom was there for me. My family and friends provided such a sense of support and connection. My mom was a teacher so she was off for the summer and was with me every step of the way. She went to every doctor appointment and always made sure that I had what I needed. I couldn't have gone through it without her there with me.

My first step was to see a surgeon. They needed to remove the underlying tumor and then inject dye to follow the path the cancer would have spread in the lymph nodes. The thought of having surgery was traumatic for me. I had never had anything like this before. I had no idea what to expect. I wanted to have an ugly mole removed and now I was going to have surgery within a week. It all seemed a little surreal.

At the eleventh hour, there was a call from the doctors to say that they wanted to run one more test so they were postponing my surgery. They wanted to be sure. While looking through my records, one of the doctors noticed that I had mentioned that the mole in question had become irritated and had bled. In an effort to be thorough and check every possibility, the doctors wanted to run another test. There was the slightest possibility that it could 'appear' to be cancer when it wasn't. Again, we waited, but the story turned out just the same. The test came back positive and my surgery was only postponed for one day.

The surgery went well. They gave me two options. Stay in the hospital or have the surgery as an outpatient. I chose to go home after my surgery. Once again, my family and friends were a great sense of strength and support for me. While the procedure itself went well, I was feeling sick and exhausted from my experience. I was thankful to have the option to leave the hospital because all I wanted to do was leave after they had finished with me. When I arrived home, the house was decorated with "Welcome Home" signs, and friends and family had baked me goodies. While I couldn't immediately enjoy the goodies, I was grateful to everyone for thinking of me.

I am thankful that my body bounced back so quickly. I spent the next week recovering and getting back to my routine and waiting. Waiting for more results. Being in college I was used to handing things over to people and waiting for evaluation, but this brought a whole new sense of anxiety. The first set of results took about a week. The surgeon called to tell us that he was able to 'get clean margins'. That meant they were able to remove the whole tumor. They ran the pathology tests and the tumor was benign!

Believe it or not, when they removed the mole, they had removed the cause of the cancer. In my mind I thought, "Well, then it couldn't have spread." Unfortunately, that's not how it works. Later that week, my mom and I made the trip to the doctor's office for the full report. When he came into the room, I could tell by his demeanor and his tone that this wasn't going to be all good news.

"We removed two lymph nodes," he said. "The path for the dye wasn't clear. Of the two we removed, one is fine and the other node contained 80% cancerous cells."

"What does that mean?" I said. I was starting to feel like this was far from over for me.

"The first thing it means for you is that you have to have another surgery. That's the biggie," he said. "It could mean that it was just one lymph node and all of the others are fine, including the second one that we removed and tested. In that case, there is a good chance that it is all out of your system."

A good chance would be great, but I still had to go through another surgery. I had to wait to have the surgery until I was completely healed from the first. This also meant a new set of doctors for me, a new surgeon and an oncologist. We were moving into a new phase. I went to a research hospital and met with an oncologist who specialized in melanoma. I felt comfortable with him immediately. Finding the surgeon became more of a fateful experience. His name had come to us through my boyfriend's parents and during my first appointment with my oncologist, he told me there was only one surgeon he worked with and it was the same surgeon. Things were moving in the right direction.

There was just one more set of tests and then the second surgery. I had been scheduled for a CT scan and a PET scan. Both of these tests look for tumors. These two tests were probably worse for me than my surgery, but I got through them. The worst part was the waiting. There are never enough things to keep you occupied when you are waiting for test results. You can pretend to watch TV or do whatever you can to keep your mind off what you are waiting for, but when it comes down to it, you are waiting for your fate.

We finally got the call late in the afternoon and both of the tests results showed that I didn't have any tumors. I was gaining some positive momentum. Now I just had to get through the second surgery and maybe this would be over. So I thought.

The second surgery was definitely a better experience than the first. I wasn't as sick afterwards from the anesthesia. The surgeon was careful with me considering what I had been through already and was able to use the previous incisions to do his work. That made it better for me to deal with all the way around. I already had two scars and I didn't want to have three or four. The recovery was going to be a little more involved for me this time.

The doctors still let me go home which was so important to me. My brother's wedding was just nine days later and I was going to be ready. I had a tube in my arm that was draining fluid from my surgery. I was determined that I was going to be at the wedding without my drainage system. I hadn't had a day to be free from my cancer and this was going to be the day. I was lucky to have the tube removed the day before the wedding.

A few days later the results were in. All of the other lymph nodes that they removed were cancer free. That was such good news. I was gaining momentum and starting to win this battle. But it wasn't over. My next step was to start the interferon alpha treatments, which is a form of chemotherapy. I was hopefully nearing the end.

My oncologist was always there to meet my needs. When I was getting ready to begin my interferon treatments, he gave me all of the information that I needed. He didn't leave anything out. Information on what the treatments would be like to go through the treatment sessions and what to expect afterwards. He even gave me phone numbers of people to call to ask questions. Once again, I felt like I had everything that I needed.

It was important to keep my life as normal as possible. Normal was busy. When I learned about the treatments from my oncologist, I was relieved that I could keep my sense of normalcy. I never gave up any of my activities. I didn't stop going to school full time, I stayed on the dance team and kept up my responsibilities to my sisters in the sorority. The more I could keep the same, the more I could feel like I was going to win.

The treatment schedule was not like traditional chemotherapy. I would be on this therapy for a full year. The first month I received the treatments through an IV in the doctor's office every day, five days a week. I had a routine. I would work in the morning, go to the doctor's office in the afternoon, sit for my IV, then go home and crawl on the couch to rest until the next day. Then I would get up and do it all over again. The treatments made me pretty sick, but I knew that I had to keep going. I was grateful to have my weekends to myself.

At the end of the first month, my regimen changed. It was the same medicine, but then it was half the dose and only three times a week. The biggest change was that I had to inject myself. There were a couple of challenges with giving myself the injections. It was difficult to get used to, but just like everything else in my life, I had to adapt. Over time, it became a challenge to find sites to give myself the injections. Luckily, I could rely on others to help me. I became everybody's pin cushion. My mom, my roommate and other volunteers. It was a team effort. The self injections lasted for the next 11 months.

I finished my interferon alpha treatments in July of 2002. Every three months I see my oncologist to make sure everything is progressing the way it should. So far, I am 100% fine. In my mind, it's finished, but in reality it will never really be over. I feel fine and I will go on living my life just like I had planned. That is one thing that I can say, I never strayed from the way I wanted to live my life.

I graduated from college in December of 2002 and am now pursuing a career in my field. It feels good to be out of school, what an accomplishment. But in a way it also feels good to have had this experience. It taught me to put things into perspective and figure out what is important. I will always be grateful to have learned those lessons.

What is our hope?

Kristin's story is an example of sheer determination. Kristin never gave up on the life that she created for herself. She believed in the goals that she set for herself and she accomplished them, one by one. She is a never-ending fountain of energy and had to use every bit of that energy and drive to focus on her life, her relationships and her disease, simultaneously. Kristin tells her story through her nature which is always positive and full of energy. Kristin proves to all of us that there is true power in a positive attitude.

. . . Rita

Nora's Story

Nora, 41, is a married, professional woman raising one son. In 1983, she was diagnosed with Type I Diabetes at the age of 21.

One of the stranger things about catching up with your disease later in life is the line of demarcation that it cuts across your personal history. Much of what I think about my life falls into either a "before" or an "after" category. The first thing I thought about when asked about my story was the reality that once there was a time when I could eat anything I wanted. For most people, eating is like breathing. No one thinks anything about it. People move throughout their day pilfering the refrigerator and grabbing a fast food snack without giving it a second thought.

That used to be me, too. I remember that.

I remember much of my life was lived without too much of a concern. I was twenty-one and married with four cats, which we treated like our babies. I had a good job and loved sports, whether it was swimming, tennis or basketball. Weekends gave us a chance to have some fun. Everything in my life was like eating and breathing. I didn't need to give much of it a second thought.

In February of 1983, I had a problem with one of my wisdom teeth and decided to bite the bullet and have it extracted. After the dentist visit, I wound up with a staff infection and even after the infection cleared up, I was still feeling dizzy. I made an appointment with my doctor to find out why the dizziness stayed around. He ran a glucose tolerance test and discovered that my levels were higher than normal.

"This happens sometimes," the doctor said. "Sometimes if you are a borderline diabetic, a shock to the body can push you over the edge. We don't necessarily understand why that happens. We just know that it does."

Looking back, I was shocked but somehow not surprised to hear the doctor's words. There was a history of diabetes in my family. My mother and all of her sisters and many of my cousins had what was referred to as "brittle diabetes". I had hoped that I might be genetically lucky and have it bounce over me.

I guess I hadn't ducked low enough.

With Type I diabetes the changes in my life were immediate. There was no time to waste. Almost immediately I would find myself sitting at work and I could feel myself starting to "bottom out". When you bottom out, your blood sugar levels drop too low. Because your body is deprived of the sugar it needs to feed your organs and function, it is hard to stay focused, or find energy or even know how to treat your symptoms because it's hard to think. It was a horrible sensation. I began to adjust my physical activities for fear that I would bottom out afterwards. It was a new worry that was completely foreign to my life.

My new lifestyle also required me to get used to monitoring myself for blood sugar levels. Everything I was beginning to experience in my body was new to me, so I wasn't able to naturally recognize early on when my sugars where dropping. All of a sudden I would be in the middle of a spinning sensation, and then I would feel very fatigued. Just that fast, my blood sugar had dropped. My morning routine which had been so automatic for so many years - get up, take a shower, get dressed and go to work - now needed to make room for me sitting on the edge of the bed each morning and checking my sugars before I even rose to my feet.

I was finding that other areas of my life needed rearranging too. I couldn't hang out with my friends in the same ways I had done for so many years. There was to be no alcohol consumption now that I was a diabetic. Many of the activities that I had participated in with my friends involved social drinking which was now off limits. That was another adjustment. I would find myself spending more and more of my time at home rather than being out socially at bars or clubs. Being at home was sometimes an easier choice for me than always having to explain the consequences of my disease or not feeling like a part of things. It didn't change my friendships, but it changed what we did for fun.

Probably the most challenging demand of my lifestyle change lay in developing confidence in my ability to monitor myself. During the early days of my disease, I was checking myself every thirty minutes. I was terrified that I might bottom out somewhere and no one would know what was wrong with me. During my first year, I was so unstable that I was even afraid to drive, for fear that I might suddenly go low behind the wheel and cause an accident. As time went on, I became more confident in my sense of what was happening to my body and whether I might be going low.

Of course, there was always the fear that my diabetes was signaling something even worse, which made the times when I would switch medications so very harried. The medications are designed to stabilize the blood sugar levels. My levels were often too high and the medications were working to bring my levels down to a more normal level. A new medication, which I wasn't familiar with, would work quickly to bring my blood sugar level down. This would sometimes trigger heart palpitations and I was concerned that I might be having a heart attack. After a few visits to the emergency room, I learned to understand those "heart wanting to leap out of your chest" moments, and they became less frightening. Every bit of the first few years was used for learning what being a diabetic was really all about.

None of my doctors were especially excited in 1998 when, at age 37, I became pregnant. They knew that my pregnancy would carry a 'high risk' tag and they didn't let me forget it. Being a high risk patient, it was important that my baby and I were monitored very closely. Every other day, I drove 45 minutes to the doctor's office to have my insulin levels tested and adjusted, if necessary. It was a small price to pay to receive the child I had always wanted. Throughout my disease, the doctors told me a pregnancy wouldn't happen. Then they told me a pregnancy couldn't happen. By some great miracle it did happen. My son is now five years old and he is as healthy as can be.

In the middle of all the demands diabetes made upon me, I found it possible to find my life again. I'm lucky to live in a time where the medications are better than they have ever been. I don't have as many ups and downs as I used to have. I am as active as any mother would be with her son. I am not afraid to do anything or go anywhere. I have developed over the years an awareness of the rhythms of my body that allows me to understand what is happening inside me at most moments.

There will always be personal adjustments to make. I still agonize that I can't eat anything that I want. I have a constant craving for sweets. I hate lugging around my test machine everywhere I go. There is never a time when I can leave it behind. It is a constant piece of luggage for me. Imagine going fishing with your husband, being in a boat and having to put down your fishing pole and bring out your tester because 'it's time'. It doesn't matter where you are or what you are doing, your body never waits for a convenient time or place. There is never a time that I can forget that I am a diabetic. There is no relief for my mind or my body.

But in the end, I have found all that I needed to make it along my journey. My endocrinologist was a godsend to me. Her patience and understanding helped me through my demanding transition. She is always willing to encourage me with new exercise routines and activities to keep me healthy and moving forward in my progress. My spouse has had to learn more about this illness than he ever imagined and backs me up twenty-four hours a day.

There are still a few mountains to climb. I am still looking for that ideal weight. At 5'4 and 134 pounds, I find myself thinking more about my weight than I should. I know that if I lower my weight, I will lower my sugars. But for the most part, I am satisfied with how I look and how I feel. I am also looking for a more stable place emotionally. I find that when I am high, I can be crabby and very edgy. I want to be able to put people around me more at ease because I am able to control the reactions I might have at any given moment.

There was a time that I thought this disease might be the death of me. As my life has turned out, there is nothing that could be said that would be farther from the truth.

What is our hope?

Nora tells us the story of managing a disease that never leaves your heart or your head. For those of us who know someone who suffers from diabetes, we know that it is a constant battle of 'balance and patience'. In Nora's story she talks about some of the frightening moments of adjustment that she went through after she was diagnosed. You can also hear beneath those words the struggle to achieve the balance of her life with the constant challenges of monitoring, dosing and managing her ups and downs with her diabetes. Nora brings us the hope that we all can live, dream and realize our dreams even in the midst of balancing our limitations.

. . . Rita

Kelly's Story

Kelly, 49, is a divorced, professional woman raising two daughters. In 1994, she was diagnosed with multiple sclerosis (MS).

Women are tougher than men. Everyone knows it. The joke is that if men had been required to bear children, there would be no babies. I think that's true. I don't know a man alive who would dare volunteer to go through labor. I worked a full day, even when I was nine months pregnant. I remember coming off an eight-hour shift at the School of Nursing when my water broke, so I walked across the street to the hospital, checked myself in, and delivered my daughter.

For me, life has always been the harder, the better.

That's why I don't think anyone was surprised when I chose health care as a profession and earned my master's degree in nursing. I went on to teach and work as a clinical specialist before I found my way to the worker's compensation industry as a case manager.

It was in 1991 that my disease began to sneak up on me. My initial symptoms were subtle and vague. My handwriting would become illegible, and sometimes my fingertips would go numb. At times, I would have the sensation that my feet were "wet." There were other times when it felt as though I could draw a line down my calf, and just beneath that line, it would feel cool. There were also times when I felt dizzy.

Being a good citizen of the medical community I started to seek help, but all I got was three years of tests and no firm answers. My results kept coming back borderline, and nobody wanted to go on record. I felt like the doctors were telling me that I was almost pregnant. It was driving me crazy. Sometimes I wished I were having a heart attack. At least that would be obvious to the people who were treating me.

One day I was speaking to a friend's sister who had MS, and I realized that every time I started to describe one of my symptoms to her, she would interrupt me and finish my sentence. I was amazed that someone else was finally speaking my language. The thrill of connecting with another person who seemed to understand was far more meaningful than the realization of what the connection might mean. She eventually suggested that I take myself to someone who specialized in MS.

In August 1994, I did just that. I went to see a doctor who specialized in the field, and the first thing he said to me was, "Why are you spending a lot of money to come down here for me to tell you what you already know?"

I thought he was joking.

"Why is it that no one will tell me what is wrong with me?" I asked.

The doctor shook his head. "Because sometimes we can't all agree on what the diagnostic criteria is supposed to be for MS."

I took a piece of paper from my purse and pushed it across his desk. "Here," I said, "Write it down for me. I want this in writing."

As his pen moved over the paper, I could see what he was writing from across the desk. An overwhelming sense of relief swept over me as I reached out and picked up what the doctor had written.

"Well, what do you know," I said softly as I read the words to myself. "I do have MS."

There is no doubt for me that living with the uncertainty about my disease was more difficult than knowing exactly what I did have. In the beginning, for about eighteen months, the speculation was that I might have amyotrophic lateral sclerosis (ALS or Lou Gehrig's disease). I had known a woman who had been diagnosed with ALS, and she had survived only three years. Whether I had ALS or not, I just needed to know what my future would look like. I'm the type of person who buys a mystery and turns immediately to the last chapter to see how it ends. For three years I lived without what I desperately needed . . . the last page in my book.

And now I knew.

At last I was free to go back and start at the beginning of my book.

My daughters were three and seven at the time I was diagnosed, so I chose not to tell them immediately. I found myself needing to keep my routine stable, and I didn't see any reason to disrupt the girls' childhood. Besides, my husband was showing that my diagnosis would be much harder on him than it was on me. Within six and a half years we were divorced, and I didn't want the children to have to process both the break-up and their mother's disease simultaneously.

My lifeline was my being able to keep in control of

my own schedule. I didn't want this thing to force me to re-arrange my life any faster than I could prevent it. I continued on with my job and kept up with all my personal activities and with my daughters' demands. It's funny, but I found the prior three years of being undiagnosed much more stressful than living with the knowledge of the actual disease. My life after the diagnosis helped me find a sort of normalcy, and I embraced it.

After nine years, I still haven't slowed down much. I am lucky. The disease hasn't progressed as rapidly as it could, so it's usually the small things that remind me that I have MS. It takes me a little longer to recover from the cold or the flu. I make the extra effort to stay in good health.

In talking to other women, I have found that many share with me the experience that the tricky things about these diseases aren't always associated with being sick. It is still terribly disappointing that my husband wasn't available to share this moment with me. At the most critical time in our marital life, he chose to disappear. He was the type of man that if it wasn't happening to him, it wasn't happening. The day I told him I had MS, he told me that he had a bad day at work. It would have been a good thing to have a partner to share my thoughts and fears and hopes with these last several years.

It's been important for me from the beginning to stay positive about where I was going with my life. One of the ways that I did that was keeping the news to myself. I didn't share the news with many people that first year because it helped me to deal with it. It is one thing to figure it out for yourself, and it's quite another to have to deal with other people's reactions as well. I wasn't sure if it would "color" how people saw me, and I didn't want to deal with that. I finally told my oldest daughter just eighteen months ago and my youngest daughter only recently.

If I had to do it all over again, I would be more aggressive about clarifying my diagnosis. Though I am intimately familiar with the health care profession, I still allowed myself to be a victim of the profession's inability at times to present the information that patients need to move on. I needed to know what was wrong with me. I should have pushed the envelope much earlier to find a diagnosis. I should have been relentless.

Knowing how the last chapter of your book may read changes your perspective on how life swirls around you. Most women are wondering about what they are going to wear to their daughter's wedding. I am wondering what mode of transportation I may be taking down the aisle. Sometimes I find myself wondering what the realities of my disease will be in the future.

I suppose that there are many more people like me than I ever imagined. People who travel through life silently bearing a burden that few may be aware of. It is important to me as I go forward to possess the insight to look past the obvious and appreciate those who live in a world few can understand.

What is our hope?

Kelly is a reflection of all of us who have faced uncertainty and needed answers. She is also an example of keeping a positive attitude and knowing your own body. We should listen to our intuition about what is going on within ourselves. Whether our symptoms are subtle or obvious, we need to search for clarity. While the search may not be easy or short, like in Kelly's case, we all need to continue to pursue the search to find the clarity we need. Any diagnosis will be filled with uncertainty, and it is extremely emotional, but it is a necessary process for all of us. It gives us the information we need to move on to whatever our next path may be.

. . . Rita

Conclusion

The amazing women that you have just read about have created a chorus of hope and inspiration with their voices. Their stories have given us themes of hope and remembrance that we can carry with us wherever the next steps of our journey may take us.

Family....Family takes on many forms in our lives, but the importance of nurturing these close relationships furthers our healing process.

Love & Support....Finding and strengthening our love and support systems to continue our lives.... because they do go on.

Commitment....Learning to make commitments to our recovery and healing, whether they are small or large. They need to be made one step at a time.

Choices....Learning to make clear choices for ourselves and our health.

Perserverance....Never giving up on our challenges.

Faith....Looking deeper into our faith for strength.

Conclusion

Energy....Tapping into our energy sources for our healing.

Spirit....Creating new ways to nourish our spirits.

Miracles....Believing in miracles....because they do happen.

Voices....Finding our voices to share our stories with others to bring them hope and inspiration....continue to strengthen the LifeLine©.

Appendix

For additional information on the diseases portrayed in this book, please visit any of the following web sites.

Breast Cancer
www.nationalbreastcancer.org: National Breast Cancer Foundation®
www.komen.org: The Susan G. Komen Breast Cancer Foundation®
www.cancer.org: American Cancer Society®

Celiac Disease
www.csaceliacs.org: Celiac Sprue Association

Crohn's Disease
www.ccfa.org: Crohn's & Colitis Foundation of America

Depression
www.nimh.nih.gov: National Institute of Mental Health

Diabetes
www.diabetes.org: American Diabetes Association®

Leukemia
www.leukemia-lymphoma.org: The Leukemia & Lymphoma Society®

Lupus
www.lupus.org: Lupus Foundation of America™

Appendix

Melanoma
www.aad.org: American Academy of Dermatology
www.cancer.org: American Cancer Society®

Multiple Sclerosis
www.nmss.org: The National Multiple Sclerosis Society®

Scleroderma
www.scleroderma.org: Scleroderma Foundation
www.slero.org: International Scleroderma Network

Stroke
www.stroke.org: National Stroke Association®
www.strokeassocation.org: American Stroke Association®

Glossary of Terms

Acute Lymphocytic Leukemia (ALL): Leukemia is defined as cancer of the bone marrow and blood. It is characterized by the uncontrolled accumulation of blood cells. Acute leukemia is a rapidly progressing disease that results in the accumulation of immature, functionless cells in the marrow and blood. The marrow often can no longer produce enough normal red blood cells, white blood cells and platelets. Anemia, a deficiency of red cells, develops in virtually all leukemia patients. The lack of normal white cells impairs the body's ability to fight infections.

Amyotrophic Lateral Sclerosis (ALS or Lou Gehrig's Disease): Amyotrophic lateral sclerosis is a motor neuron disease. Motor neuron diseases are progressive chronic diseases of the nerves, which come from the spinal cord that are responsible for supplying electrical stimulation to the muscles. This stimulation is necessary for the movement of body parts.

ALS is progressive and fatal. The usual causes of death of patients with motor neuron diseases are not directly related to the disease, but result from simultaneous additional illnesses, which ultimately occur because of weakness of the body. These illnesses are often infections. ALS occurs most often in adults in the fifth through seventh decades of life. It progressively leads to death in 2 to 7 years. The cause is unknown.

Anemia: The condition of having less than the normal number of red blood cells or less than the normal quantity of hemoglobin in the blood. The oxygen-carrying capacity of the blood is therefore decreased.

Angiogram: An x-ray of blood vessels, which can be seen because the patient receives an injection of dye to outline the vessels on the x-ray.

Basal Cell Carcinoma: Basal cell carcinoma is a form of skin cancer. It is the most common form of skin cancer and accounts for 90% of all skin cancer cases in the US.

Blood Transfusion: A blood transfusion is the transfer of blood or blood products from one person (donor) into another person's bloodstream (recipient).

Bone Marrow: The soft material in the center of bones is the bone marrow. In some bones, the bone marrow consists only of fat. Other bones contain what is termed cellular marrow. The cellular marrow has different types of cells that give rise to red cells, white cells and platelets. The marrow may also contain abnormal cells that are not usually present, such as cancer cells. Since the production of red cells requires iron, the marrow is one of the places in the body that normally stores a supply of iron.

Bone Marrow (Aspiration) Biopsy: A bone marrow procedure (commonly referred to as a bone marrow biopsy or bone marrow aspiration) is a technique used to obtain the blood-forming portion (marrow) of the inner core of bone for examination in the laboratory or for transplantation. The bone marrow consists of inserting a special needle into a bone that contains marrow and withdrawing the marrow by suction or coring out a sample of the marrow.

CT (CAT) Scan: A computed tomography (CT) scan is a special type of X-ray that can produce detailed pictures of structures inside the body. A CT scan is also called a computerized axial tomography (CAT) scan.

Celiac Sprue (Celiac Disease): Celiac sprue is a condition whereby the absorption of food nutrients through the small intestine is impaired because of an immune (allergic) reaction to gluten. The small intestine is the part of the digestive tract where the absorption of nutrients occurs. The adult human small intestine is an elongated tube measuring up to twenty-two feet. It is located between the stomach and the large intestine (colon). Gluten is a protein found in wheat or related grains, and is present in many foods that we eat. Celiac sprue is generally reversible once certain grains or products of grains (such as beer) are removed from the diet.

Celiac sprue is also called nontropical sprue, gluten enteropathy, or adult celiac disease: The condition is seen in people in all parts of the world. The highest incidence appears to occur in Ireland where nearly one out of every three hundred people is afflicted. It was not until as recently as 1950 that gluten in the diet was associated with this disease.

Chemotherapy: Drug therapy for cancer. Also called "chemo" for short. Most anticancer drugs are given IV (into a vein) or IM (into muscle). Some anticancer agents are taken orally (by mouth). Chemotherapy is usually systemic treatment, meaning that the drugs flow through the bloodstream to nearly every part of the body.

Patients who need many rounds of IV chemotherapy may receive the drugs through a catheter (a thin flexible tube). One end of the catheter is placed in a large vein in the chest. The other end is outside the body or attached to a small device just under the skin.

<u>*Colon:*</u> The part of the large intestine that runs from the cecum to the rectum as a long hollow tube that serves to remove water from digested food and lets the remaining material, solid waste called stool, move through it to the rectum and leave the body through the anus.

<u>*Crohn's Disease:*</u>   Crohn's disease is a chronic inflammatory disease of the intestines. It primarily causes ulcerations (breaks in the lining) of the small and large intestines, but can affect the digestive system anywhere from the mouth to the anus. It is named after the physician who described the disease in 1932. It also is called granulomatous enteritis or colitis, regional enteritis, ileitis, or terminal ileitis.

<u>*Cystic Fibrosis:*</u> One of the most common grave genetic (inherited) diseases, CF affects the exocrine glands and is characterized by the production of abnormal secretions, leading to mucous build-up.

This accumulation of mucus can impair the pancreas and, secondarily, the intestine. Mucous build-up in the lungs tends progressively to impair respiration. Without treatment, CF results in death for 95% of affected children before age 5. However, with diligent medical care patients with CF are surviving even beyond middle age.

Dermatologist: A doctor who specializes in the diagnosis and treatment of skin problems.

Diabetes Mellitus, Type I: An autoimmune disease that occurs when T cells attack and decimate the beta cells in the pancreas that are needed to produce insulin so that the pancreas makes too little insulin (or no insulin). Without the capacity to make adequate amounts of insulin, the body is not able to metabolize blood glucose (sugar) to use it efficiently for energy, and toxic acids (called ketoacids) build up in the body. There is a genetic predisposition to type 1 diabetes.

The disease tends to occur in childhood, adolescence or early adulthood (before age 30) but it may have its clinical onset at any age. The symptoms and signs of type 1 diabetes characteristically appear abruptly, although the damage to the beta cells may begin much earlier and progress slowly and silently.

Diabetes Mellitus, Type II: One of the two major types of diabetes, the type in which the beta cells of the pancreas produce insulin but the body is unable to use it effectively because the cells of the body are resistant to the action of insulin. Although this type of diabetes may not carry the same risk of death from ketoacidosis, it otherwise involves many of the same risks and complications as does type 1 diabetes (in which there is a lack of insulin).

The aim of treatment is to normalize the blood glucose in an attempt to prevent or minimize complications. People with Type II diabetes may experience marked hyperglycemia, but most do not require insulin injections. In fact, 80% of all people with Type II diabetes can be treated with diet, exercise, and if need be, oral hypoglycemic agents (drugs taken by mouth to lower the blood sugar).

Diabetes Mellitus, "Brittle": A type of diabetes when a person's blood glucose (sugar) level often swings quickly from high to low and from low to high. Also called "unstable diabetes" or "labile diabetes."

Dysthymia: A type of depression involving long-term, chronic symptoms that may not be disabling, but keep a person from functioning at "full steam" or from feeling good. Dysthymia is a less severe type of depression than what is accorded the diagnosis of major depression. However, people with dysthymia may also sometimes experience major depressive episodes, suggesting that there is a continuum between dysthymia and major depression.

Electrocardiogram (EKG): A recording of the electrical activity of the heart. An electrocardiogram is a simple, non-invasive procedure. Electrodes are placed on the skin of the chest and connected in a specific order to a machine that, when turned on, measures electrical activity all around the heart. Output is usually in the form of a long scroll of paper displaying a printed graph of activity. Newer models output the data directly to a computer and screen, although a printout may still be made.

Endocrinologist: A medical endocrinologist is a physician who specializes in the diagnosis and management of hormone conditions. Endocrinology is often paired with the study of diabetes and metabolism.

Endoscopy: Endoscopy is a broad term used to describe examining the inside of the body using an lighted, flexible instrument called an endoscope. In general, an endoscope is introduced into the body through a natural opening like the mouth or anus. Although endoscopy can include examination of other organs, the most common endoscopic procedures evaluate the esophagus (swallowing tube), stomach, and portions of the intestine.

Gastroenterologist: A doctor who specializes in diagnosing and treating diseases of the digestive system.

Gluten: A protein found in wheat and/or related grains.

Gynecologist: A doctor who specializes in treating diseases of the female reproductive organs. The word "gynecologist" comes from the Greek gyno, gynaikos meaning woman + logia meaning study, so a gynecologist is literally a student of women, a women's doctor.

Hematologist: A physician who is specially trained in the diagnosis, treatment, and prevention of diseases of the blood and bone marrow as well as the immunologic, hemostatic (blood clotting) and vascular systems.

Hemoglobin: Hemoglobin is the protein molecule in red blood cells which carries oxygen from the lungs to the body's tissues and returns carbon dioxide from the tissues to the lungs. The iron contained in hemoglobin is responsible for the red color of blood.

Hydrocephalus: Hydrocephalus is an abnormal accumulation of cerebrospinal fluid (CSF) in the brain. The fluid (the CSF) is often under increased pressure, which can compress (squeeze) and damage the brain. Hydrocephalus is sometimes familiarly called "water on the brain."

Insulin: A natural hormone made by the pancreas that controls the level of the sugar glucose in the blood. Insulin permits cells to use glucose for energy. Cells cannot utilize glucose without insulin.

Lyme Disease: Lyme disease is a bacterial illness caused by a bacterium called a "spirochete." Ticks spread Lyme disease when they bite the skin. Lyme disease can cause abnormalities in the skin, joints, heart and nervous system.

Lymph Nodes: One of many small rounded masses of lymphatic tissue surrounded by a capsule of connective tissue, located throughout the lymphatic system. The lymph nodes filter lymph (lymphatic fluid) and store special cells that can trap cancer cells or bacteria that are traveling through the body in lymph. The lymph nodes are the main source of lymphocytes of the blood. Also called a lymph gland.

__Magnetic Resonance Imaging (MRI):__   Magnetic resonance imaging (MRI) is a test that provides pictures of organs and structures inside the body. It produces these images by using a magnetic field and pulses of radio wave energy. In many cases, MRI provides information that cannot be obtained from X-ray tests.

__Mammogram:__ An X-ray of the breast with the breast in a device that compresses and flattens it. There are two basic mammogram tests — screening mammograms and diagnostic mammograms.

A screening mammogram is one performed on women who have no signs of breast cancer. It usually involves two X-rays of each breast. The aim of a screening mammogram is to detect a tumor that cannot be felt. Most mammograms that are performed are screening mammograms.

A diagnostic mammogram takes longer and involves correspondingly more radiation exposure than a screening mammogram because it involves more X-rays.

Diagnostic mammograms are done to evaluate:

· Abnormalities that have seen or suspected on a prior screening mammogram;

· Subjective or objective abnormalities in the breast such as a lump, pain, thickening, nipple discharge or a inexplicable change in breast size or shape;

· Breasts for which it is difficult to obtain a clear X-ray by a screening mammogram because of special circumstances such as breast implants.

Mastectomy: General term for removal of the breast, usually to remove cancerous tissue. The operation can be done in a hospital or in an outpatient clinic, depending on how extensive it needs to be. It takes from two to three hours, with three to five weeks for full recovery.

Melanoma: The most dangerous form of skin cancer, a malignancy of the melanocyte, the cell that produces pigment in the skin. Melanoma is most common in people with fair skin, but can occur in people with all skin colors. Most melanomas present as a dark, mole-like spot that spreads and, unlike a mole, has an irregular border.

Multiple Sclerosis: Multiple sclerosis (MS) was first described in Holland by a 14th century physician. It is a disease in which the nerves of the central nervous system (brain and spinal cord) degenerate. Myelin, which provides a covering or insulation for nerves, improves the conduction of impulses along the nerves and also is important for maintaining the health of the nerves. In MS, inflammation causes the myelin to degenerate and eventually disappear. Consequently, the electrical impulses that travel along the nerves decelerate. Late in the disease, the nerves themselves are damaged. As more and more nerves are affected, a patient experiences a progressive interference with functions that are controlled by the nervous system such as vision, speech, walking, writing, and memory.

About 250,000 to 350,000 people in the U.S. have MS. Usually, a patient is diagnosed with MS between 20 and 40 years of age, but MS has been diagnosed as early as age 15 and as late as age 60. MS is twice as likely to occur in Caucasians as in any other group. Women are twice as likely as men are to be affected by MS earlier in life. Later in life, the incidence of the disease in men and women is almost equal.

Nephrologist: A physician who specializes in the care of the kidney.

Neurologist: A physician who specializes in the diagnosis and treatment of disorders of the nervous system.

Neurosurgeon: A physician trained in surgery of the nervous system and who specializes in surgery on the brain and other parts of the nervous system.

Oncologist: A physician who specializes in the diagnosis and treatment of cancer.

Oophorectomy: The removal of one or both ovaries by surgery. Also known as ovariectomy.

Orthopedic Surgeon: A physician trained in the surgical treatment of the skeletal system (bones).

Parkinson's Disease: A slowly progressive neurologic disease characterized by a fixed inexpressive face, a tremor at rest, slowing of voluntary movements, a gait with short accelerating steps, peculiar posture and muscle weakness, caused by degeneration of an area of the brain called the basal ganglia, and by low production of the neurotransmitter dopamine. Most patients are over 50, but at least 10 percent are under 40.

PET Scan: Positron emission tomography (PET), a highly specialized imaging technique using short-lived radioactive substances. This technique produces three-dimensional colored images.

PET scanning provides information about the body's chemistry not available through other procedures. Unlike CT (computerized tomography) or MRI (magnetic resonance imaging), which look at anatomy or body form, PET studies metabolic activity or body function. PET has been used primarily in cardiology, neurology, and oncology. In particular, it has been used to assess the benefit of coronary artery bypass surgery, identify causes of childhood seizures and adult dementia, and detect and grade tumors. It is very sensitive in picking up active tumor tissue but does not measure the size of it.

Peripheral Neuropathy: A condition, which is outlined by dysfunction of the nerves outside the spinal cord. Symptoms may include numbness, weakness, burning pain (especially at night), and loss of reflexes.

Platelet: An irregular, disc-shaped element in the blood that assists in clotting. During normal blood clotting, the platelets clump together (aggregate). Although platelets are often classed as blood cells, they are actually fragments of large bone marrow cells called megakaryocytes.

Polymyositis: A chronic inflammatory disease of muscle that begins when white blood cells, the immune cells of inflammation, spontaneously invade muscles, especially the muscles closest to the trunk or torso, resulting in sometimes severe muscle pain, tenderness and weakness.

Prosthesis: An artificial substitute or replacement of a part of the body such as a tooth, eye, a facial bone, the palate, a hip, a knee or another joint, the leg, an arm, etc. A prosthesis is designed for functional or cosmetic reasons or both.

Rheumatologist: A physician who specializes in the non-surgical treatment of rheumatic illnesses, especially arthritis.
Sciatic Nerve: The largest nerve in the body, the sciatic nerve begins from nerve roots in the lumbar part of the spinal cord (in the low back) and extends through the buttock area to send nerve endings down to the legs.

Scleroderma: Scleroderma is a connective tissue disease that primarily affects the skin. For reasons unknown, parts of the skin become thick and hard. Similar changes can occur in other organs, including the lungs, heart, kidneys, and gastro-intestinal tract.

There are two major types of scleroderma:

· Localized scleroderma — This type of scleroderma is diagnosed when only the skin and muscles are involved.

· Systemic scleroderma — This type of scleroderma is diagnosed when organs other than the skin and muscles are involved. This form of scleroderma is more properly known as "systemic sclerosis."

Shunt: 1) To move a body fluid, such as cerebrospinal fluid, from one place to another. 2) A catheter (tube) that carries cerebrospinal fluid from a ventricle in the brain to another area of the body. A shunt may be placed to relieve pressure from hydrocephalus, for example.

Spinal Tap (Lumbar Puncture): A spinal tap (lumbar puncture or LP) is a procedure whereby spinal fluid is removed from the spinal canal for the purpose of diagnostic testing. It is particularly helpful in the diagnosis of inflammatory diseases of the central nervous system, especially infections, such as meningitis. It can also provide clues to the diagnosis of stroke, spinal cord tumor and cancer in the central nervous system.

Stroke: The sudden death of some brain cells due to a lack of oxygen when the blood flow to the brain is impaired by blockage or rupture of an artery to the brain. A stroke is also called a cerebrovascular accident or, for short, a CVA.

Symptoms of a stroke depend on the area of the brain affected. The most common symptom is weakness or paralysis of one side of the body with partial or complete loss of voluntary movement or sensation in a leg or arm. There can be speech problems and weak face muscles, causing drooling. Numbness or tingling is very common. A stroke involving the base of the brain can affect balance, vision, swallowing, breathing and even unconsciousness.

Stent: A tube designed to be inserted into a vessel or passageway to keep it open. Named after Charles R. Stent (1845-1901), an English dentist.

Systemic Lupus Erythematosus (SLE): A chronic inflammatory condition caused by an autoimmune disease. Patients with lupus have unusual antibodies in their blood that are targeted against their own body tissues.

Lupus can cause disease of the skin, heart, lungs, kidneys, joints, and nervous system. When only the skin is involved, the condition is called discoid lupus. When internal organs are involved, the condition is called systemic lupus erythematosus (SLE). Up to 10% of persons with discoid lupus (lupus limited to the skin) eventually develop the systemic form of lupus (SLE).

SLE is eight times more common in women than men. The causes of SLE are unknown.

Order Information

For more information about upcoming books in the LifeLines© Series. . .

To place an on-line order for additional copies of LifeLines©: Stories from Women with Hope . . .

To add to the voices and share your story. . .

For additional background on the author and other resource information . . .

Please visit www.lifelines-stories.com